SPACE COLORING BOOK FOR KIDS AGES 6-10

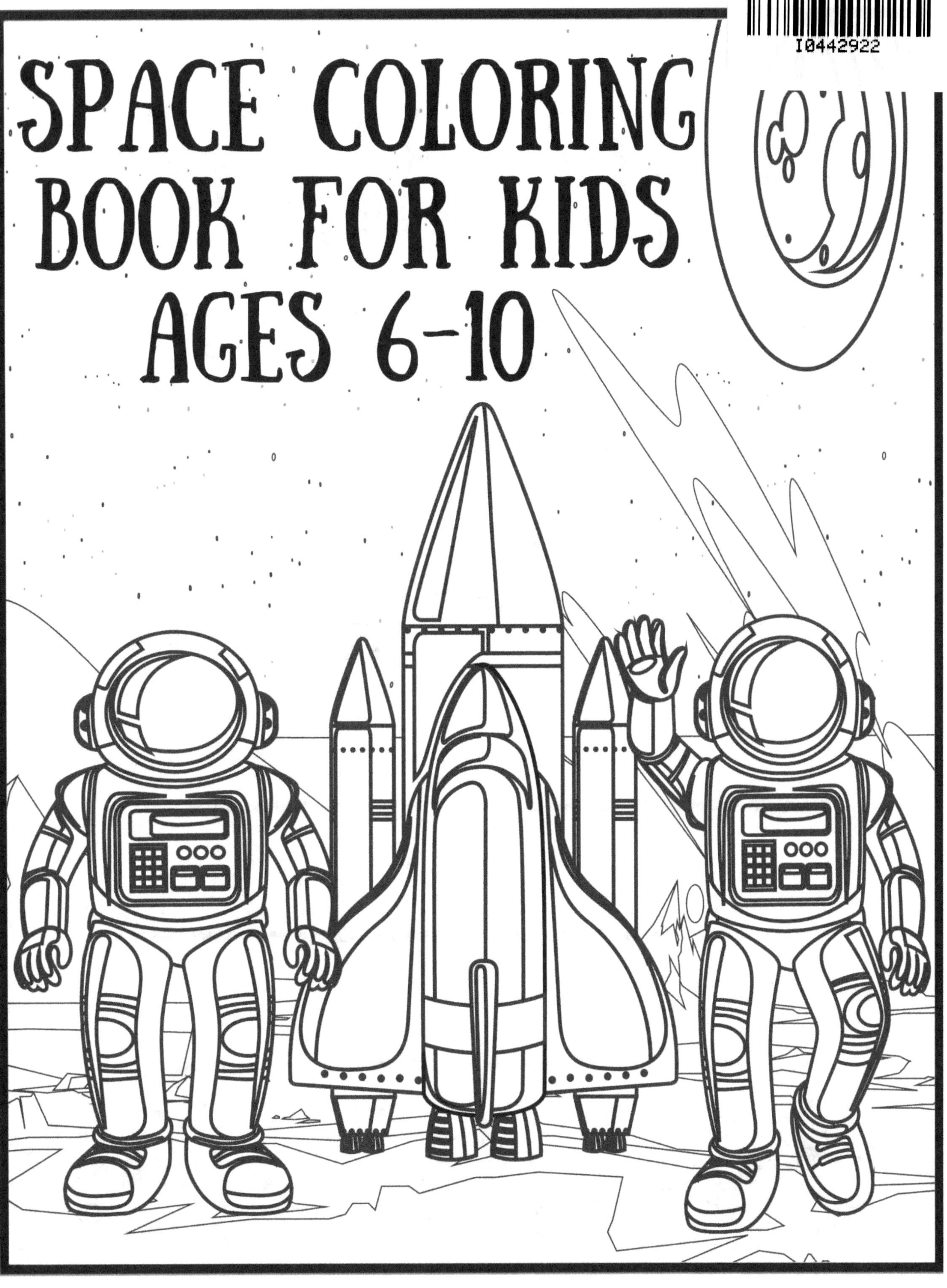

THIS BOOK BELONGS TO

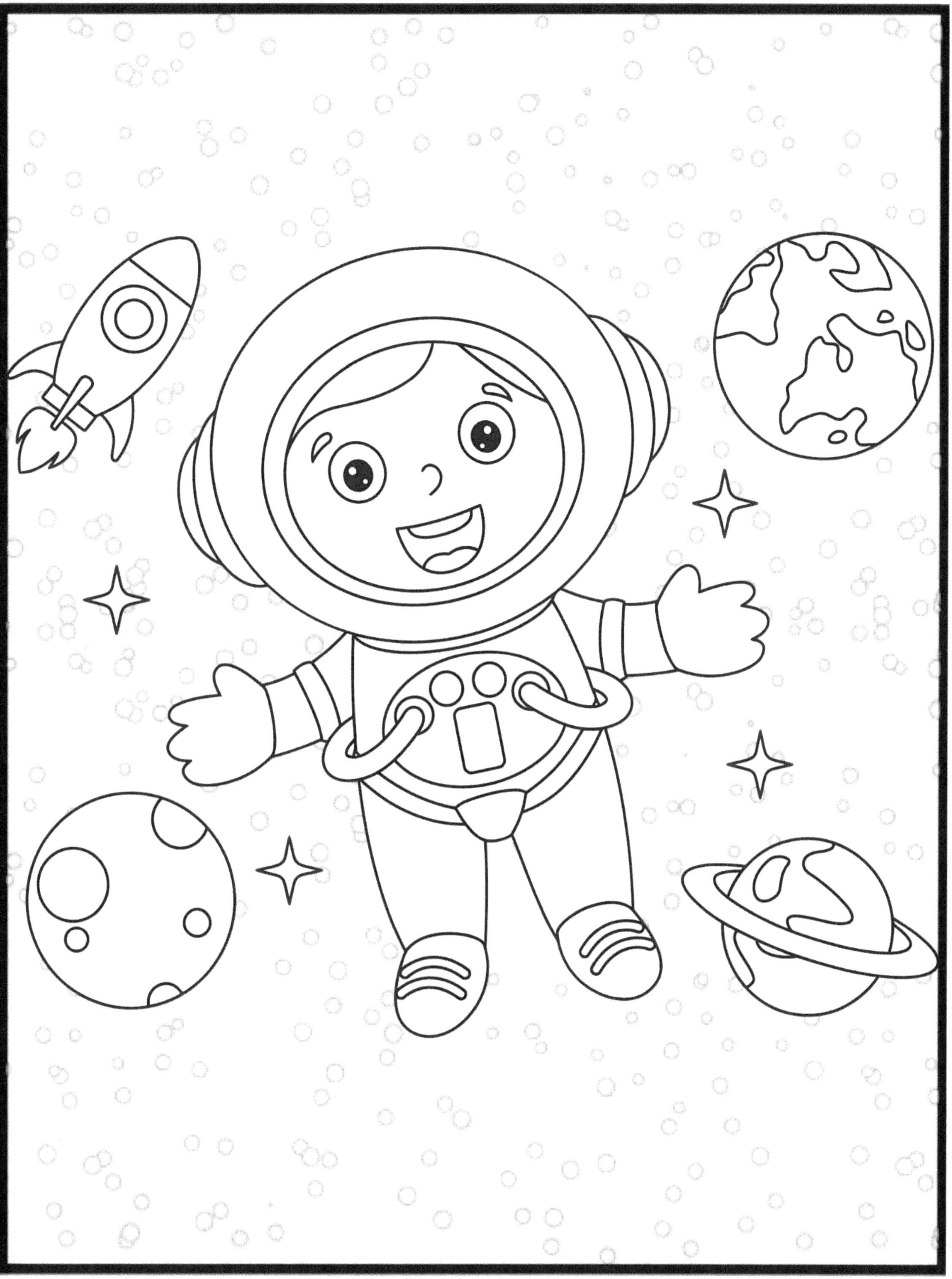

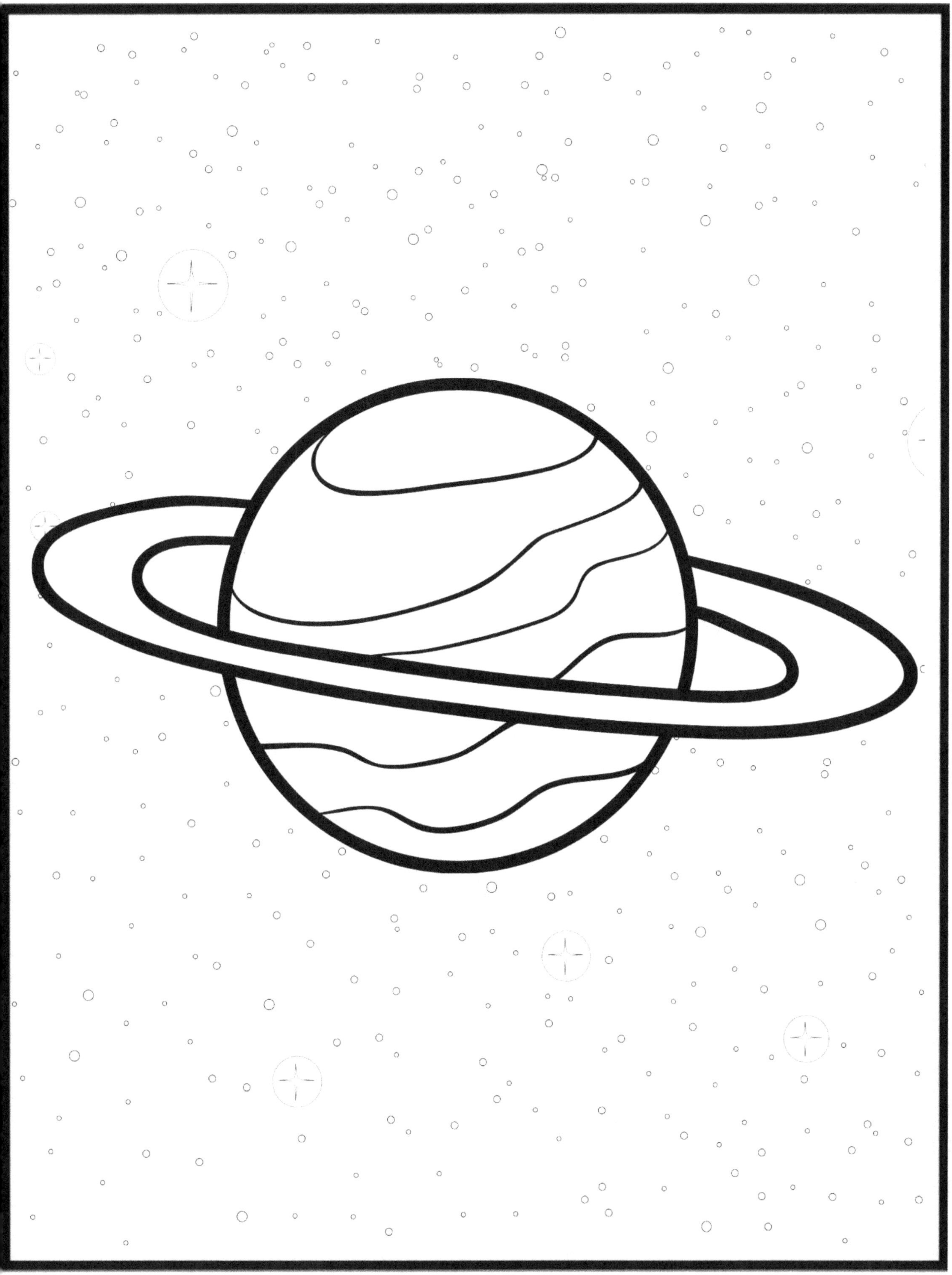

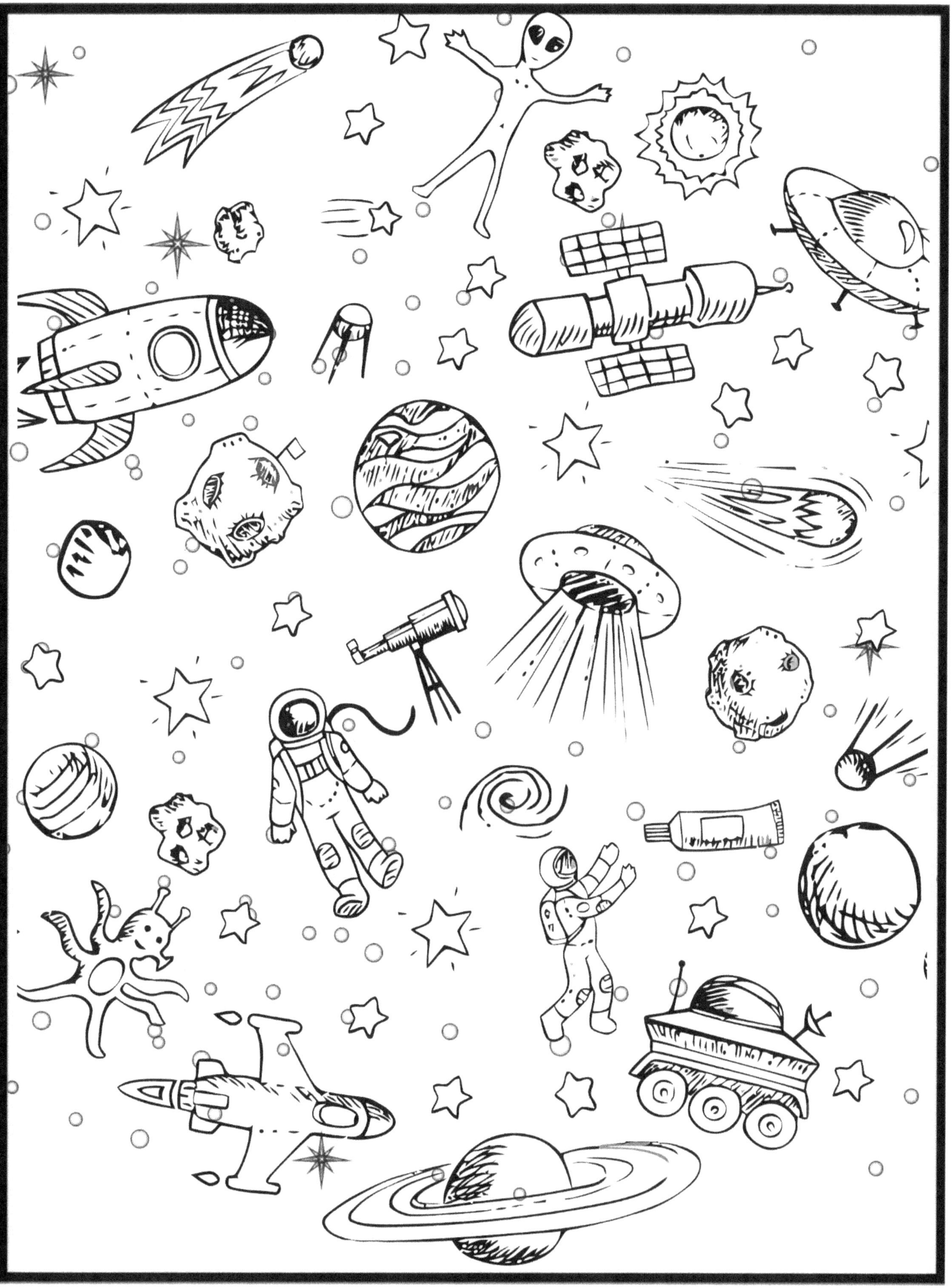

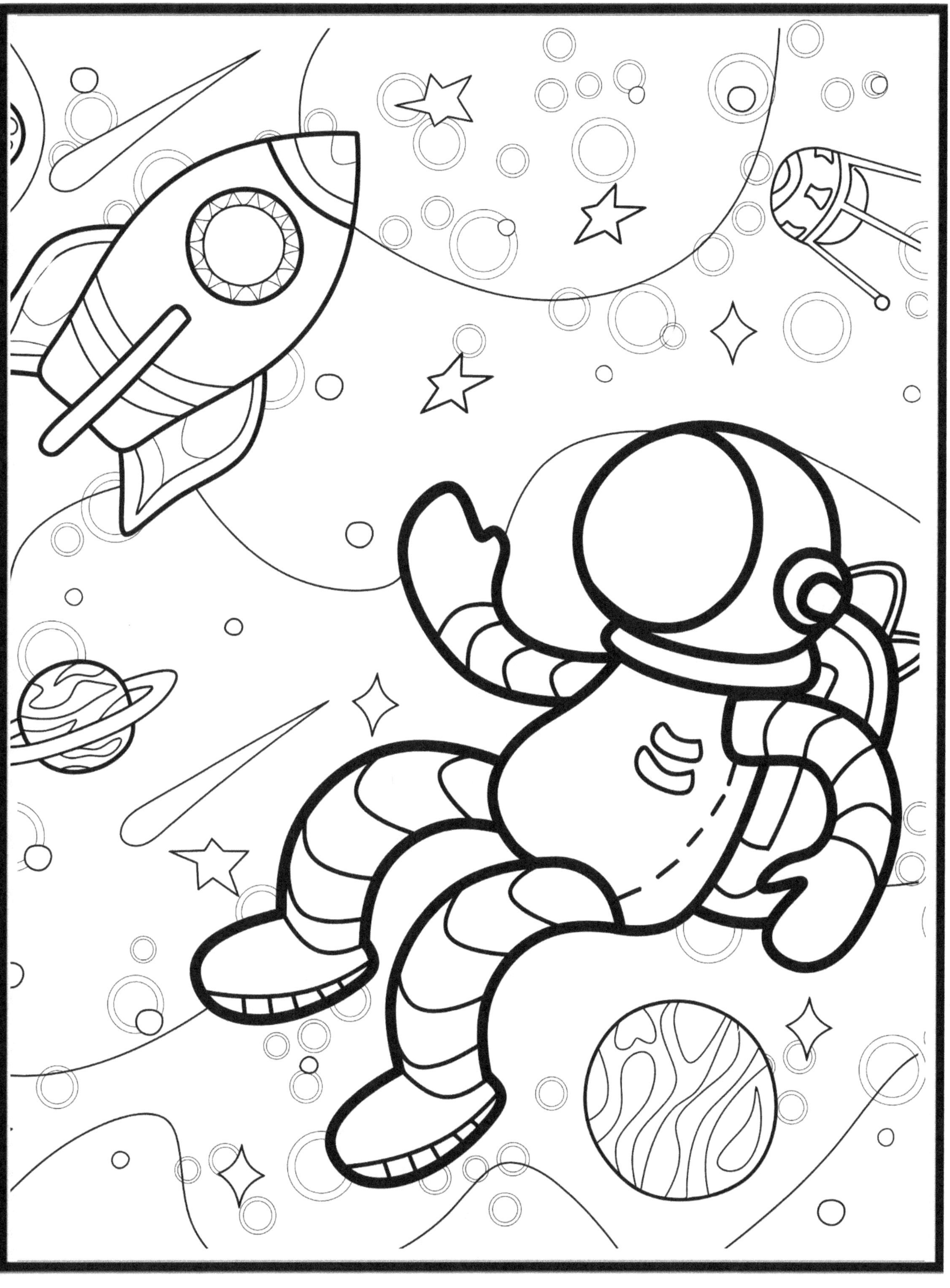

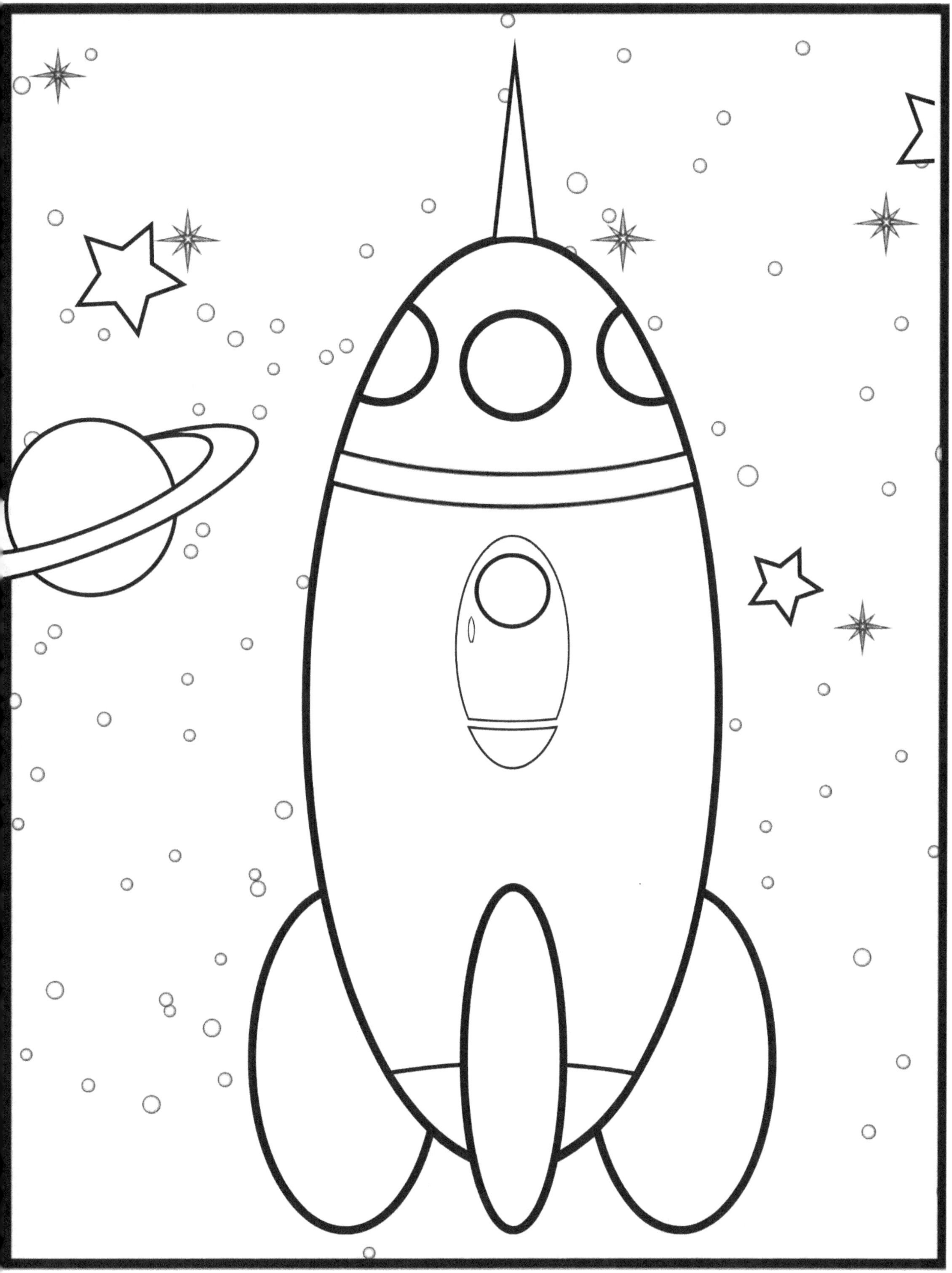

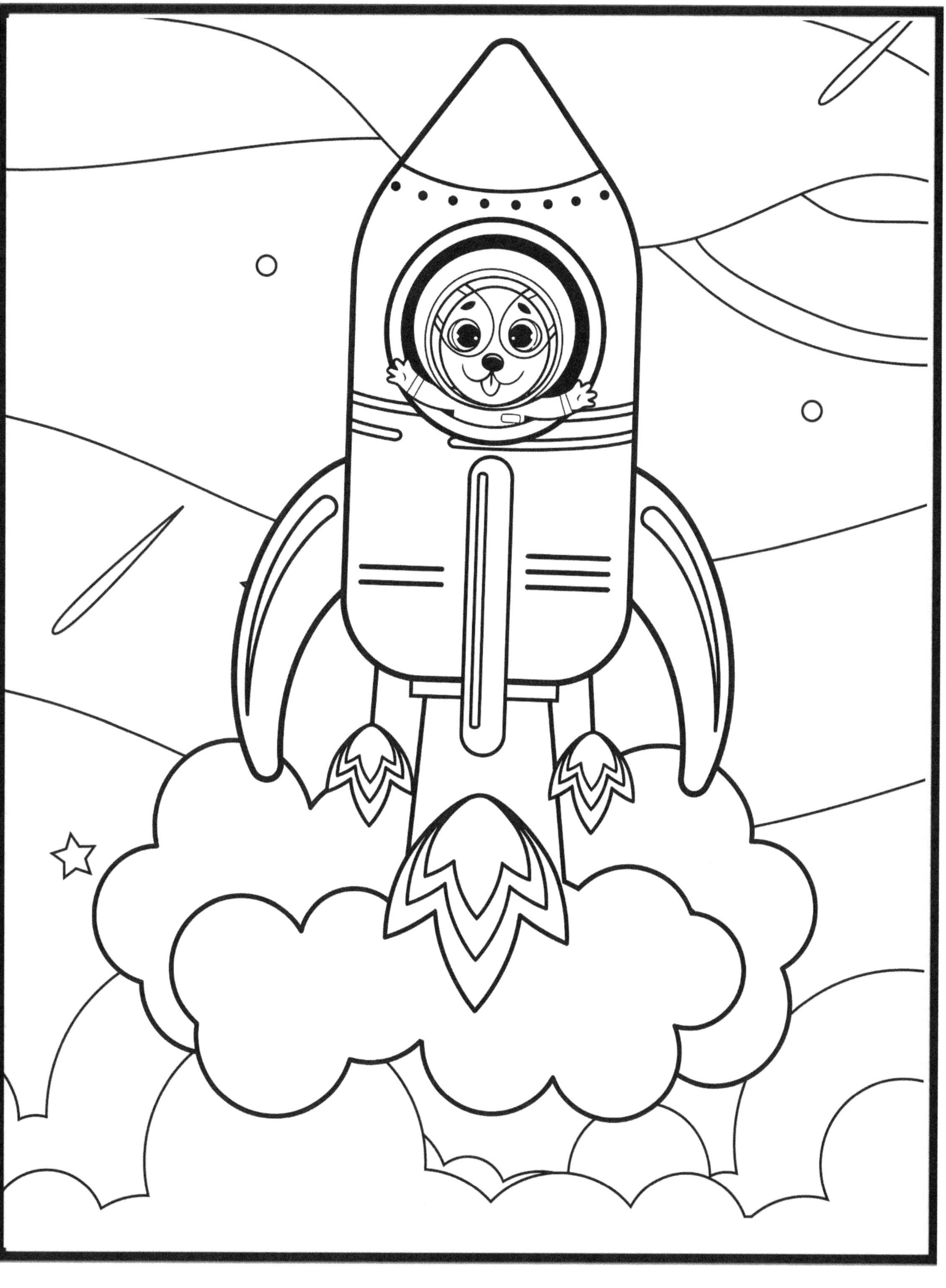

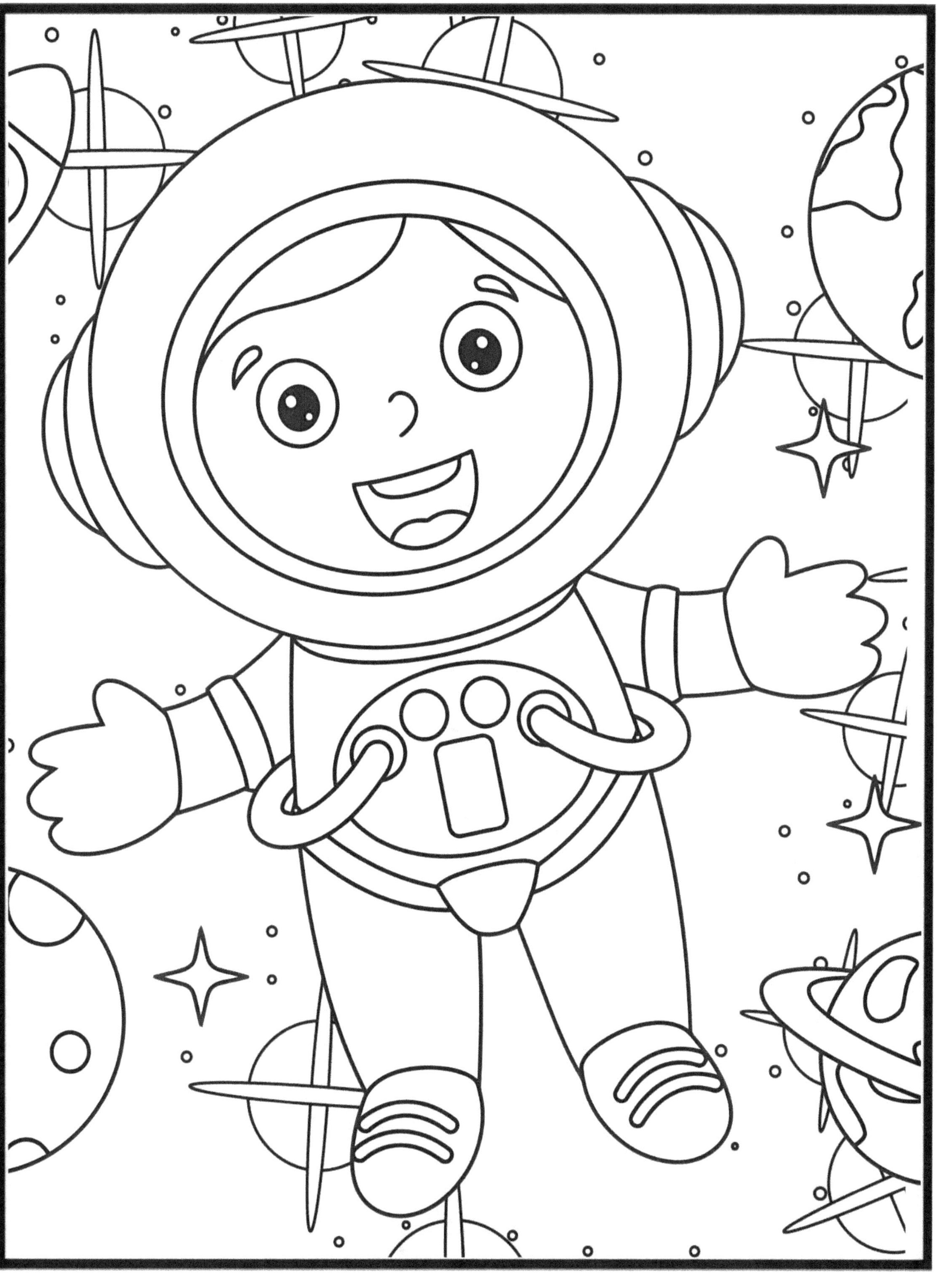

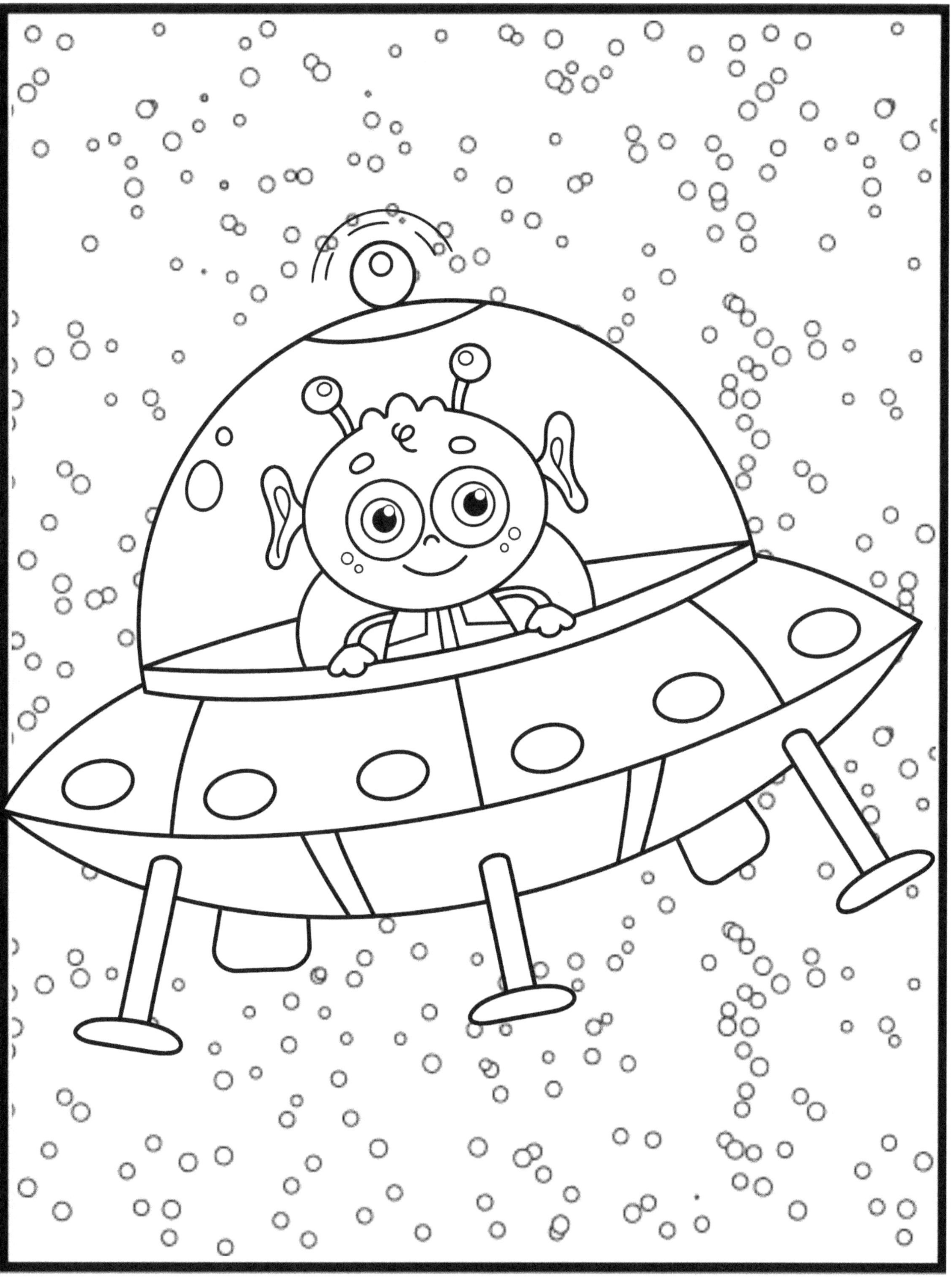

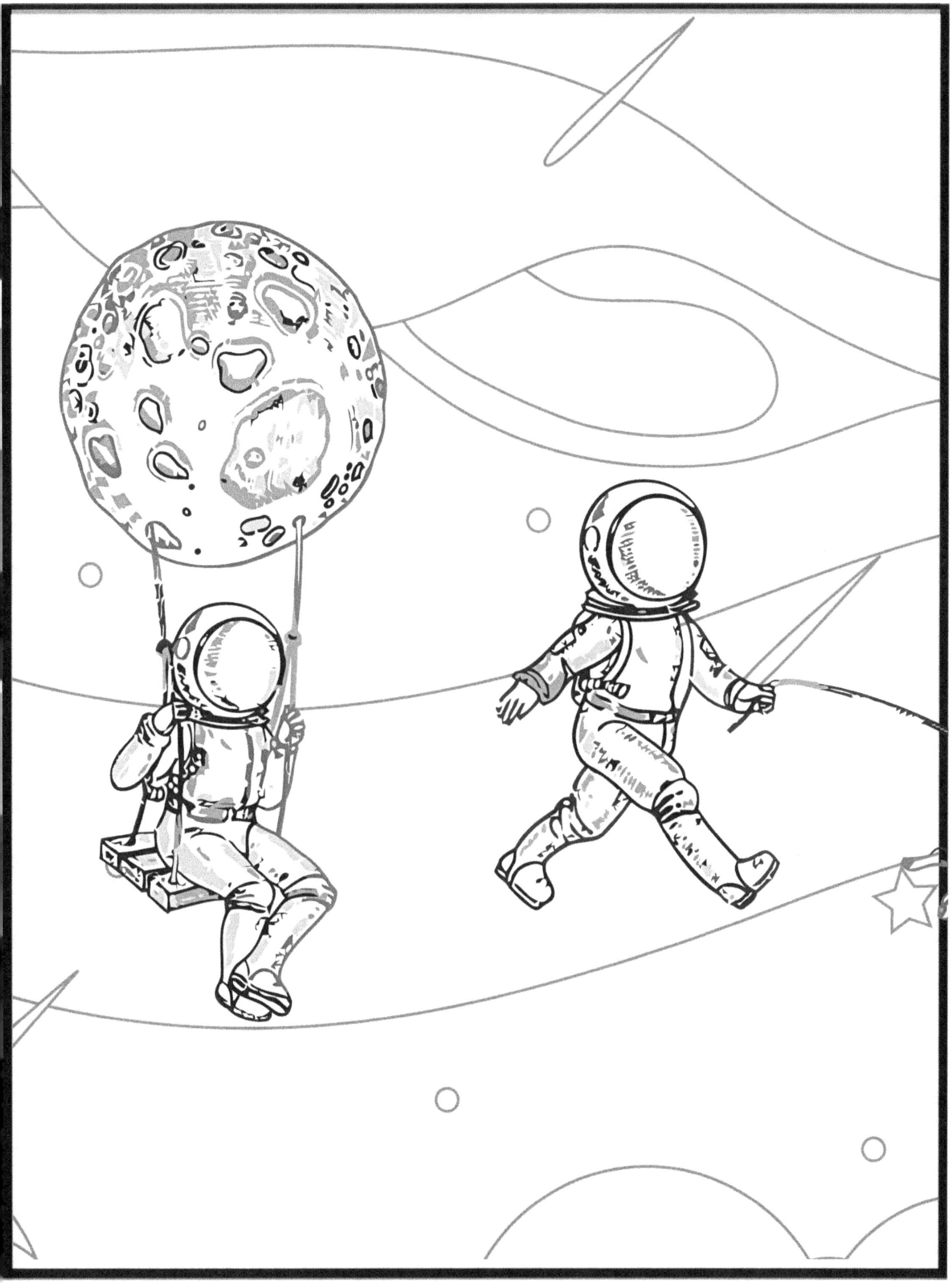

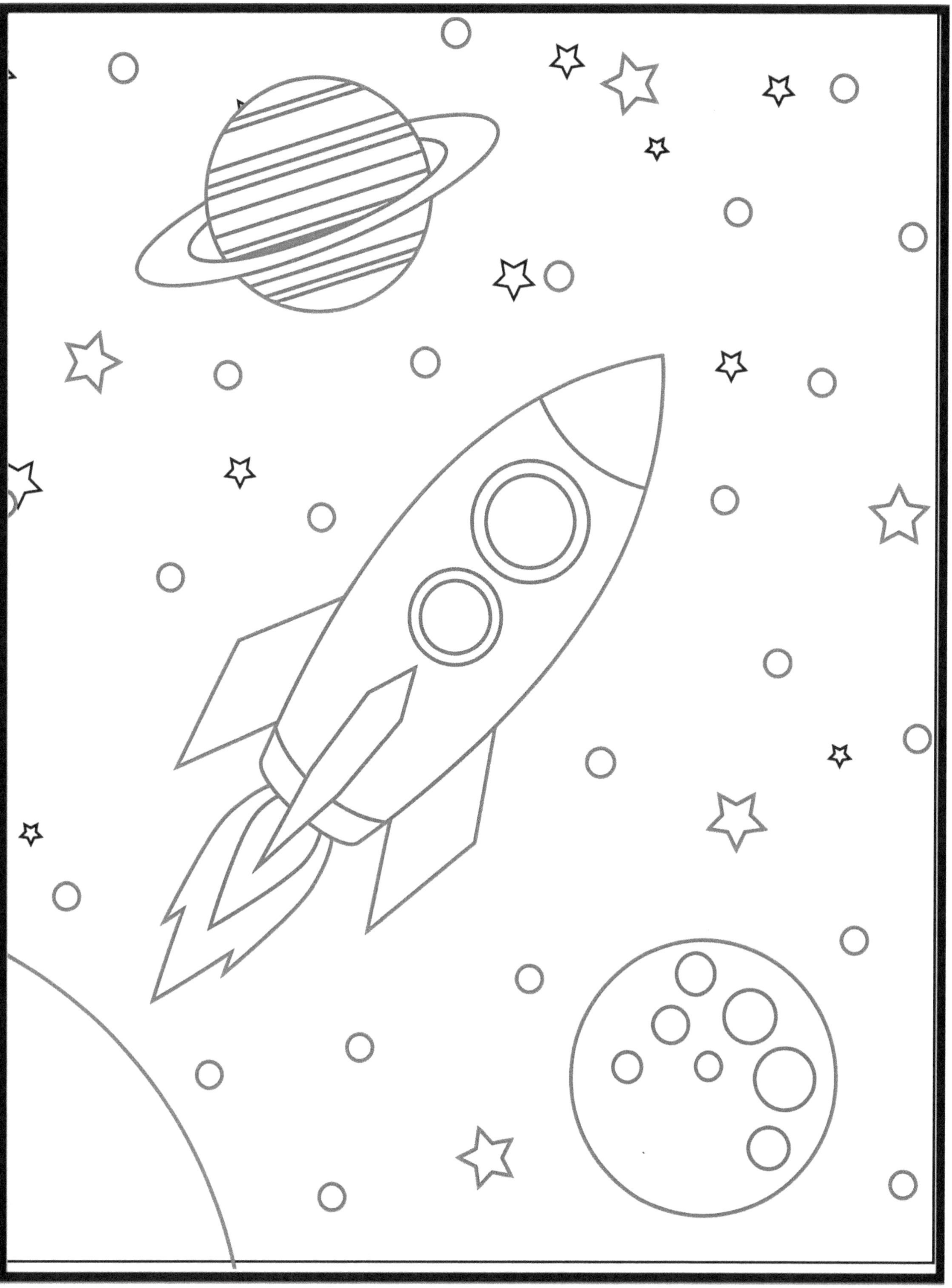

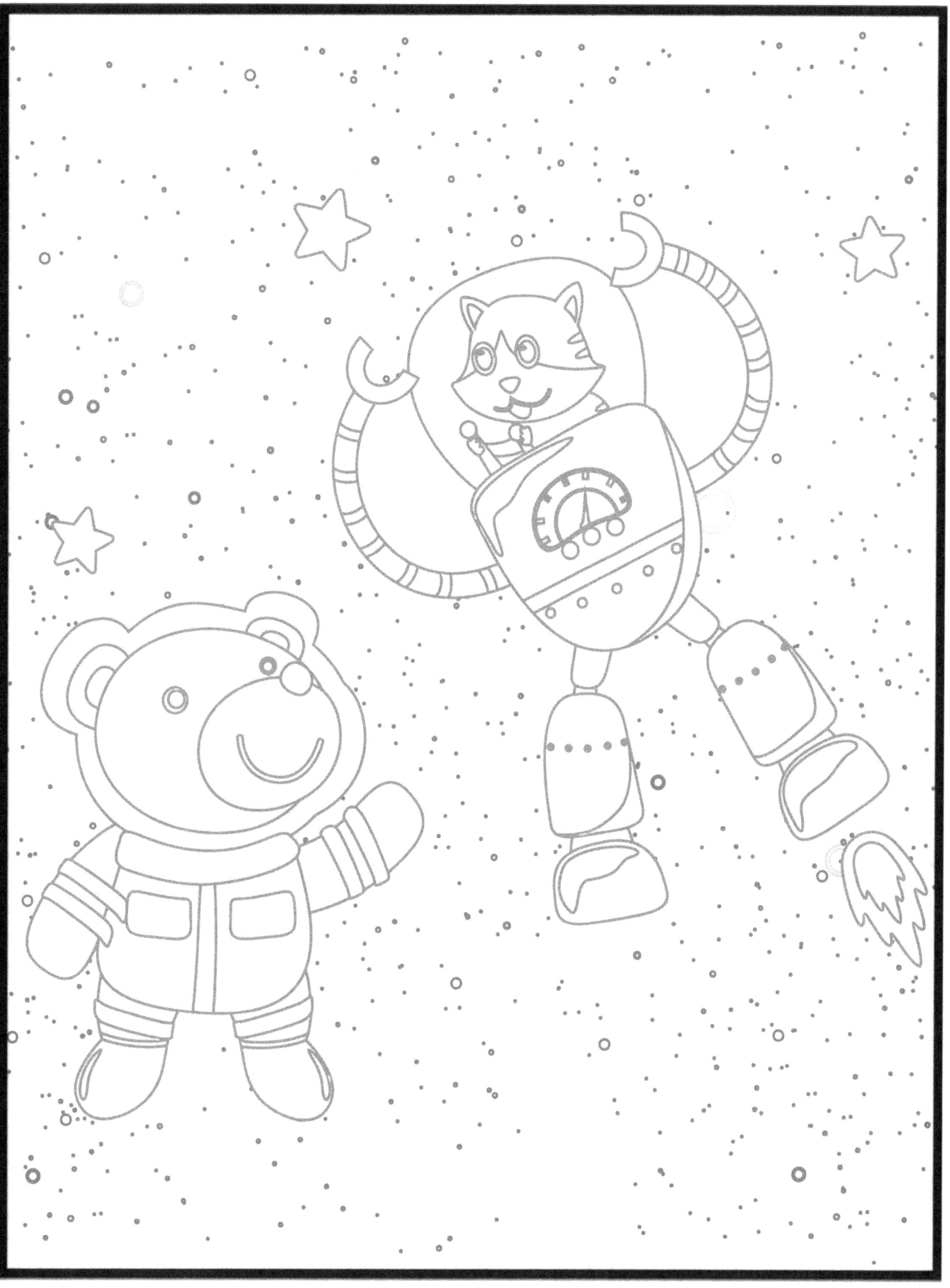

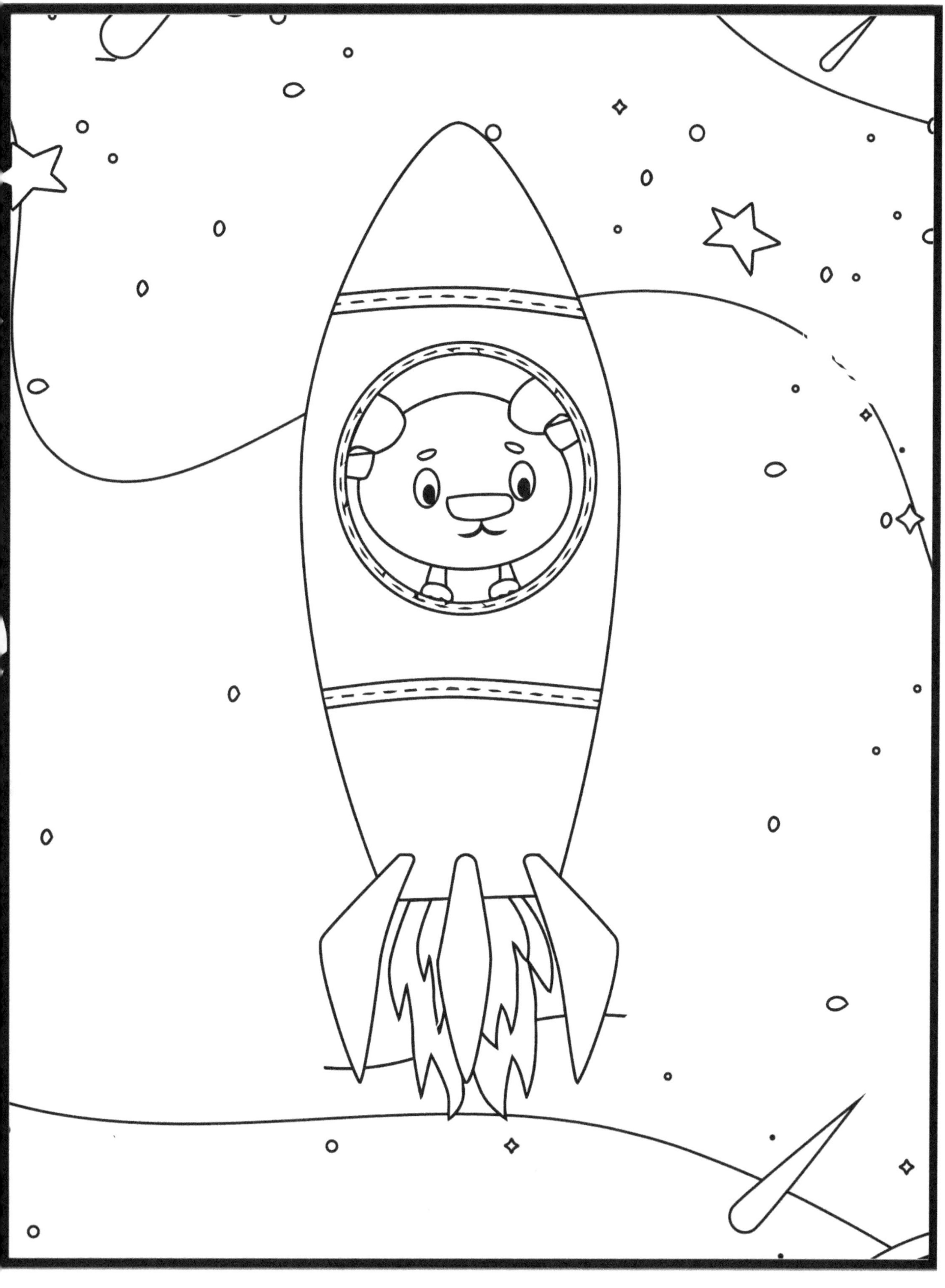

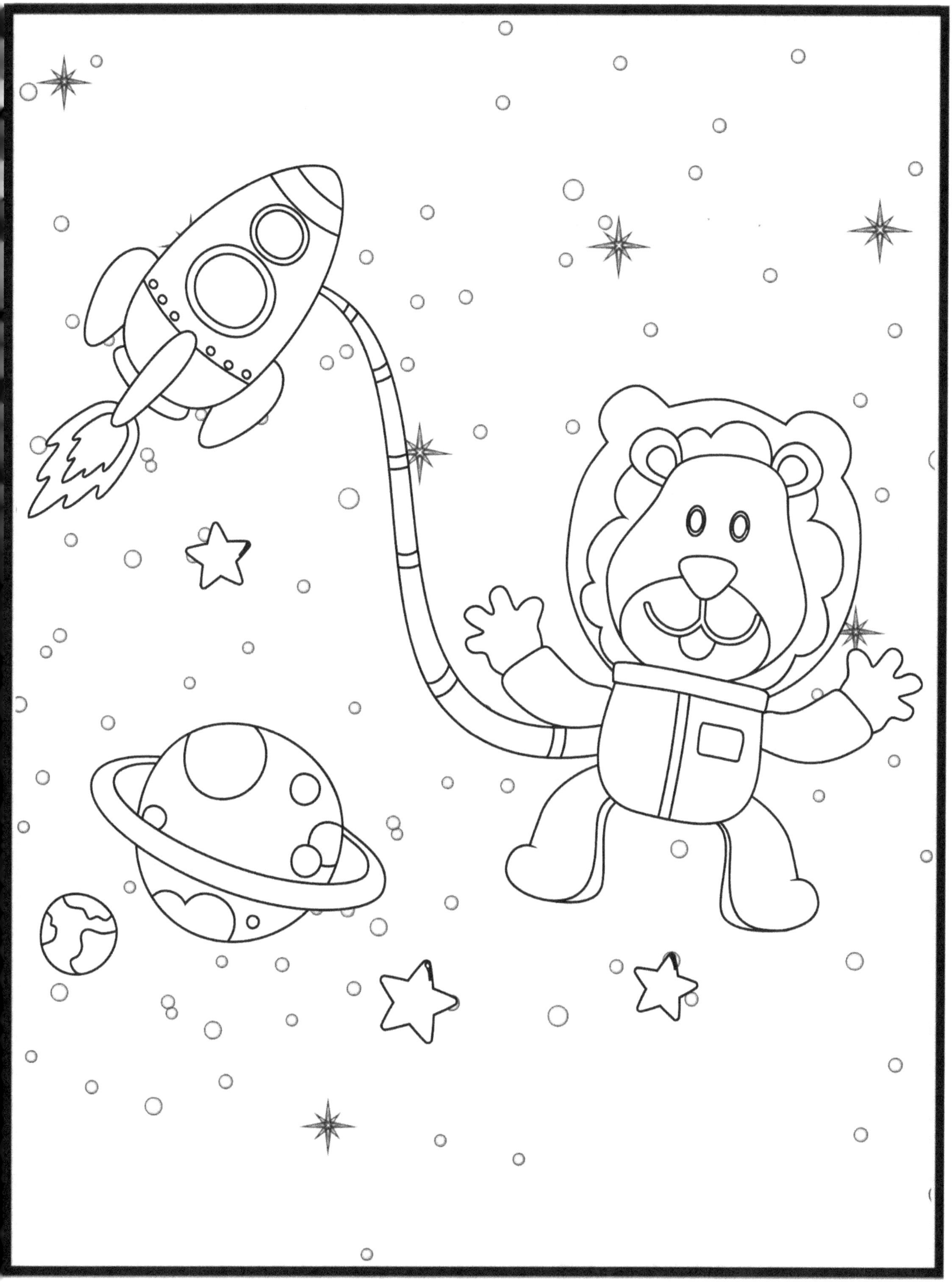

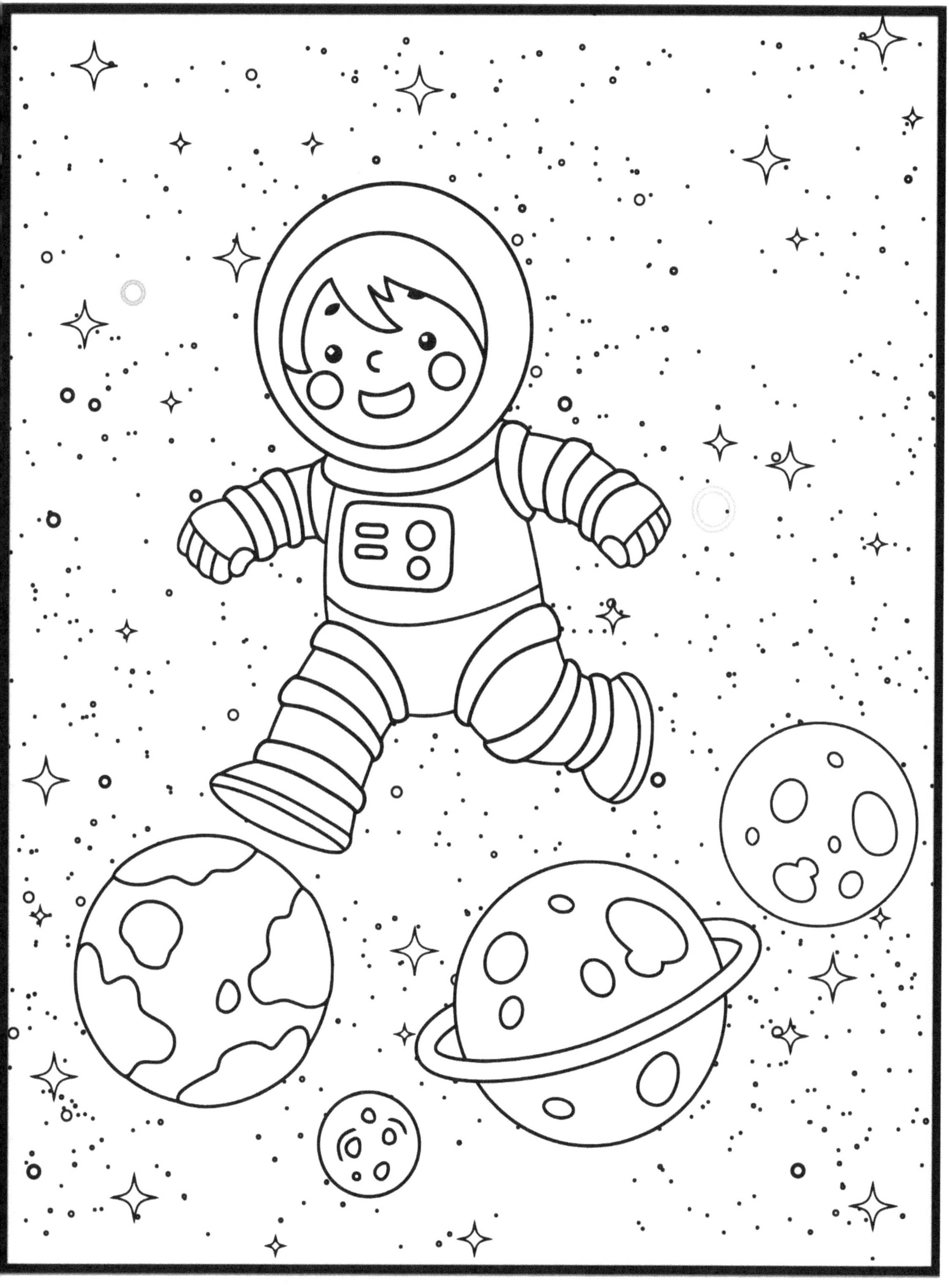

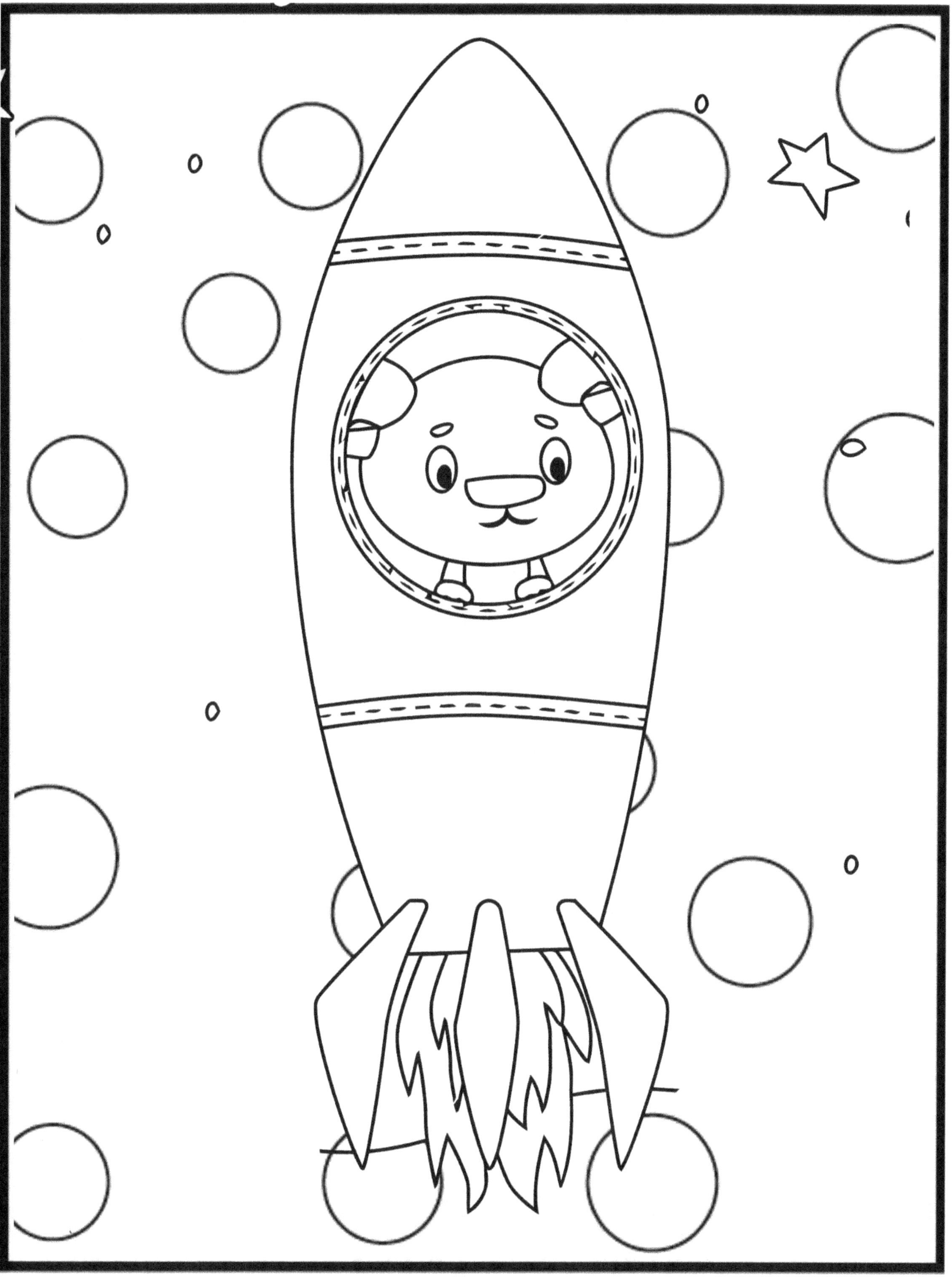

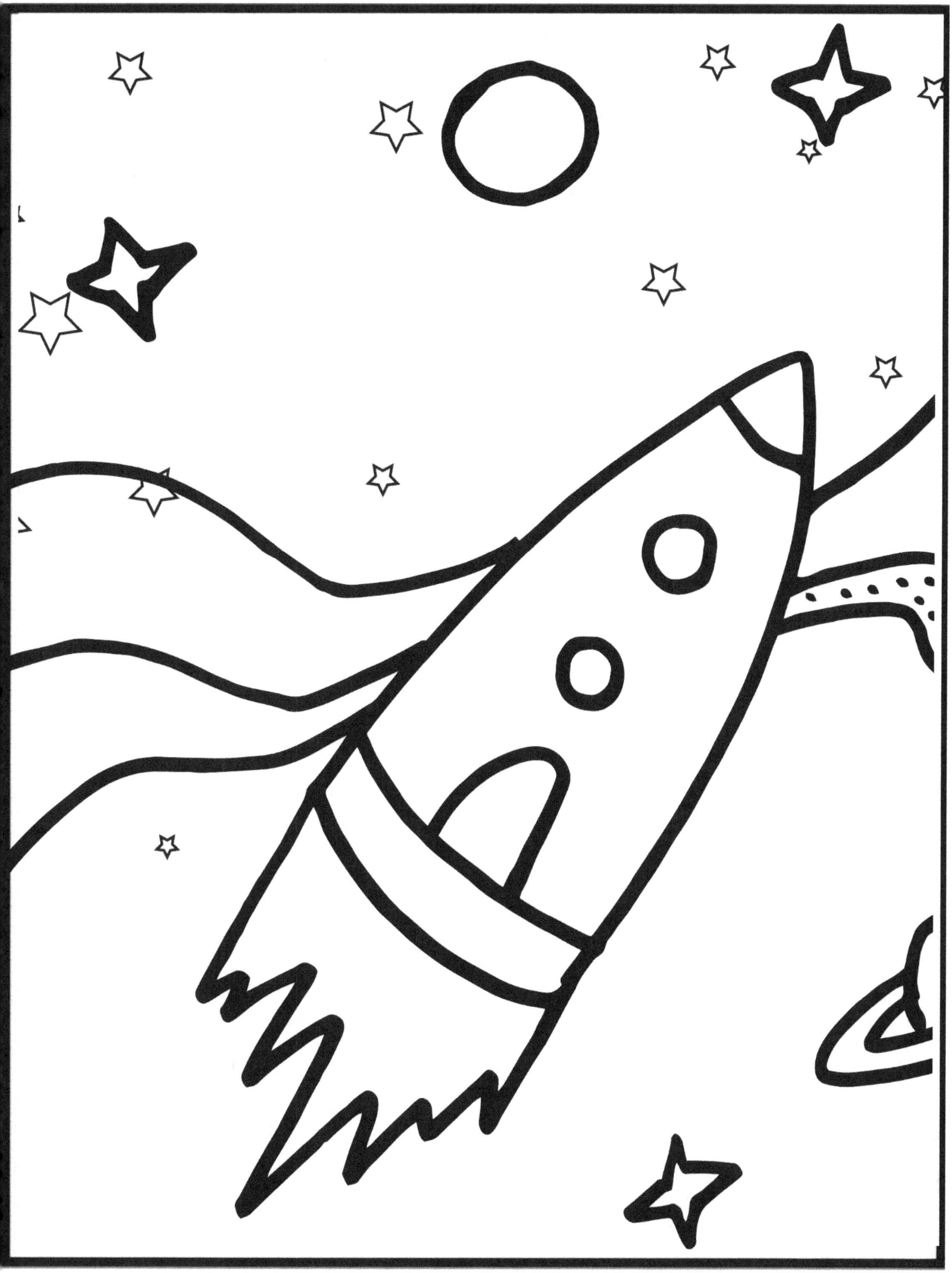

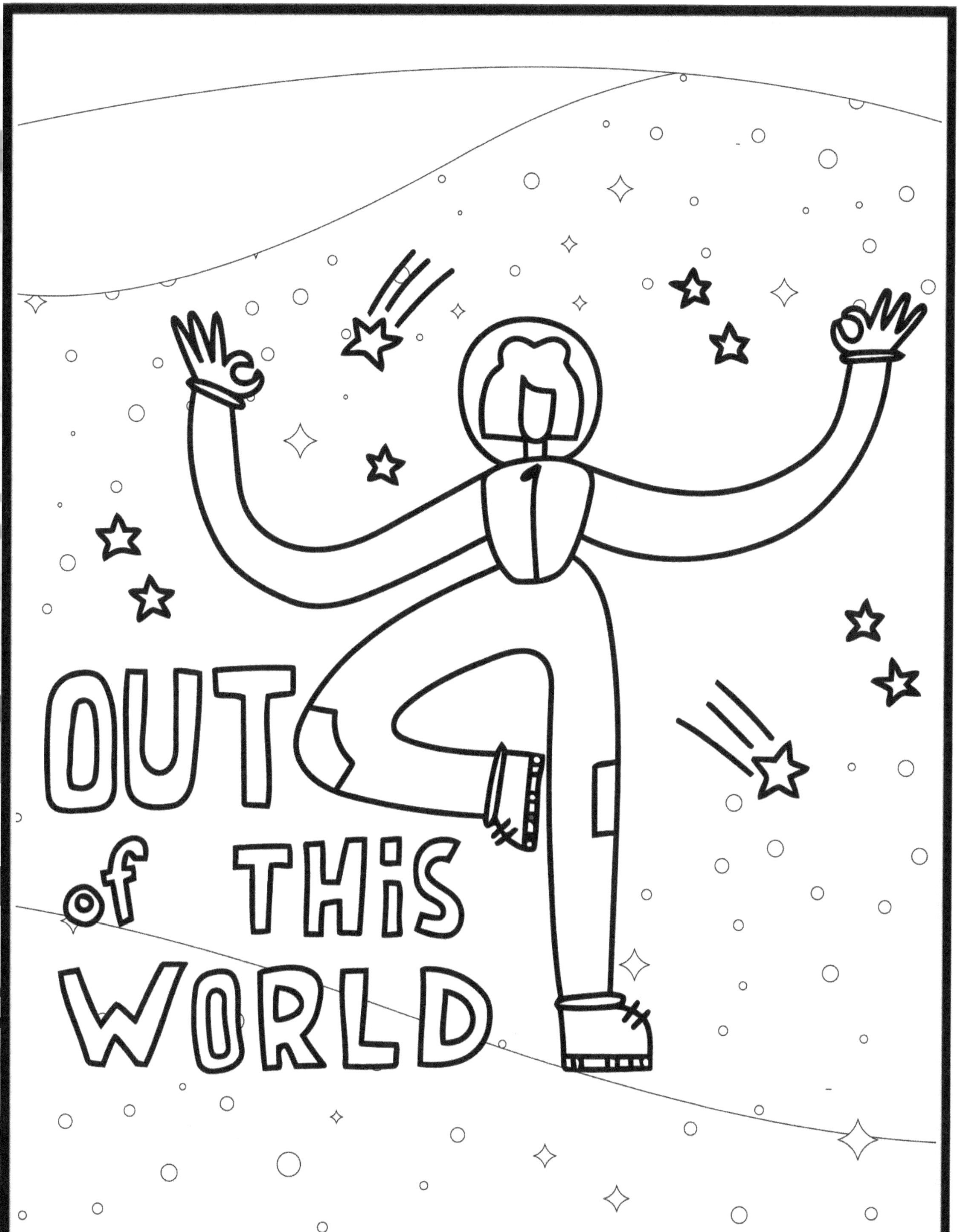
OUT
of THIS
WORLD

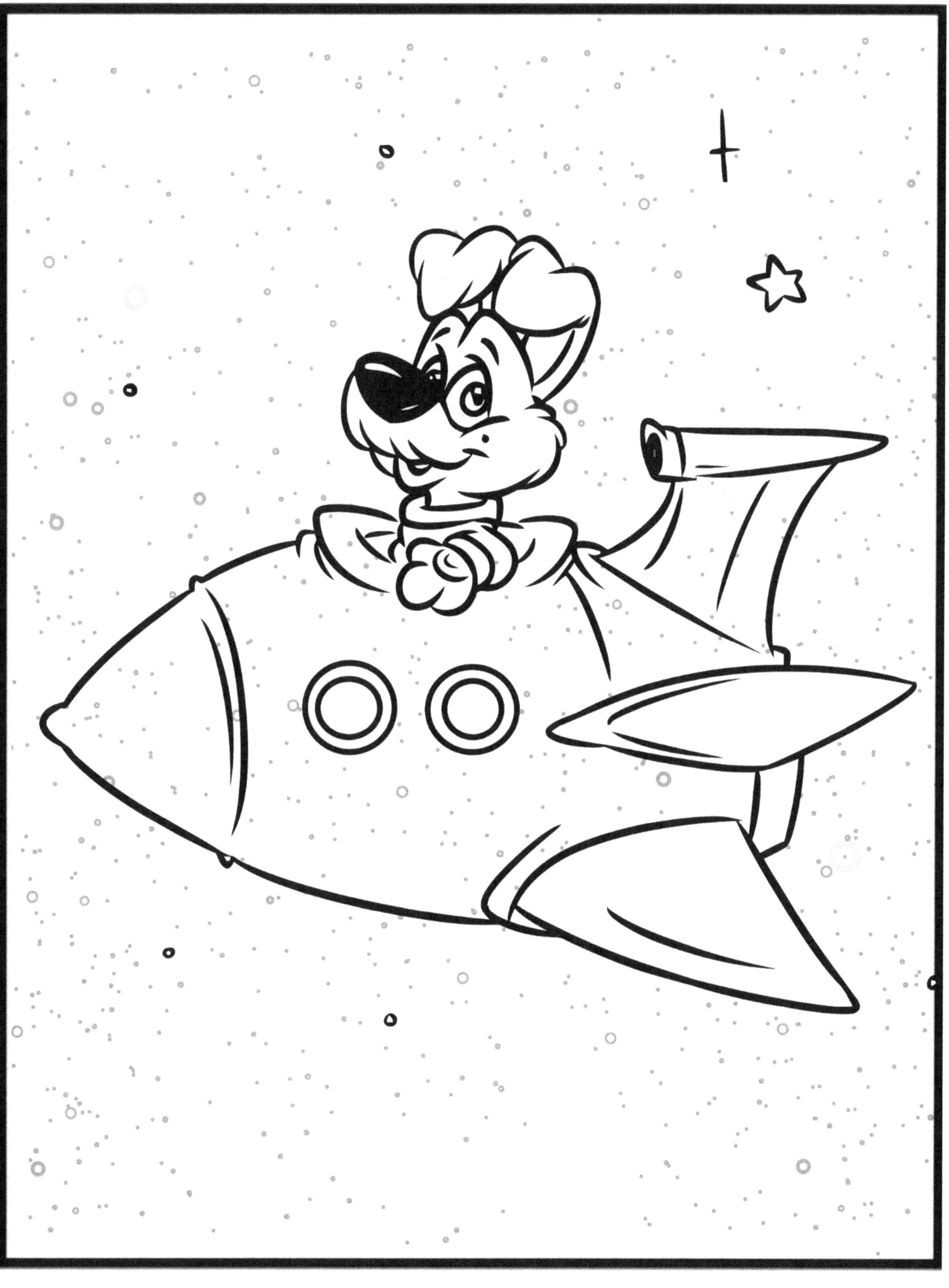

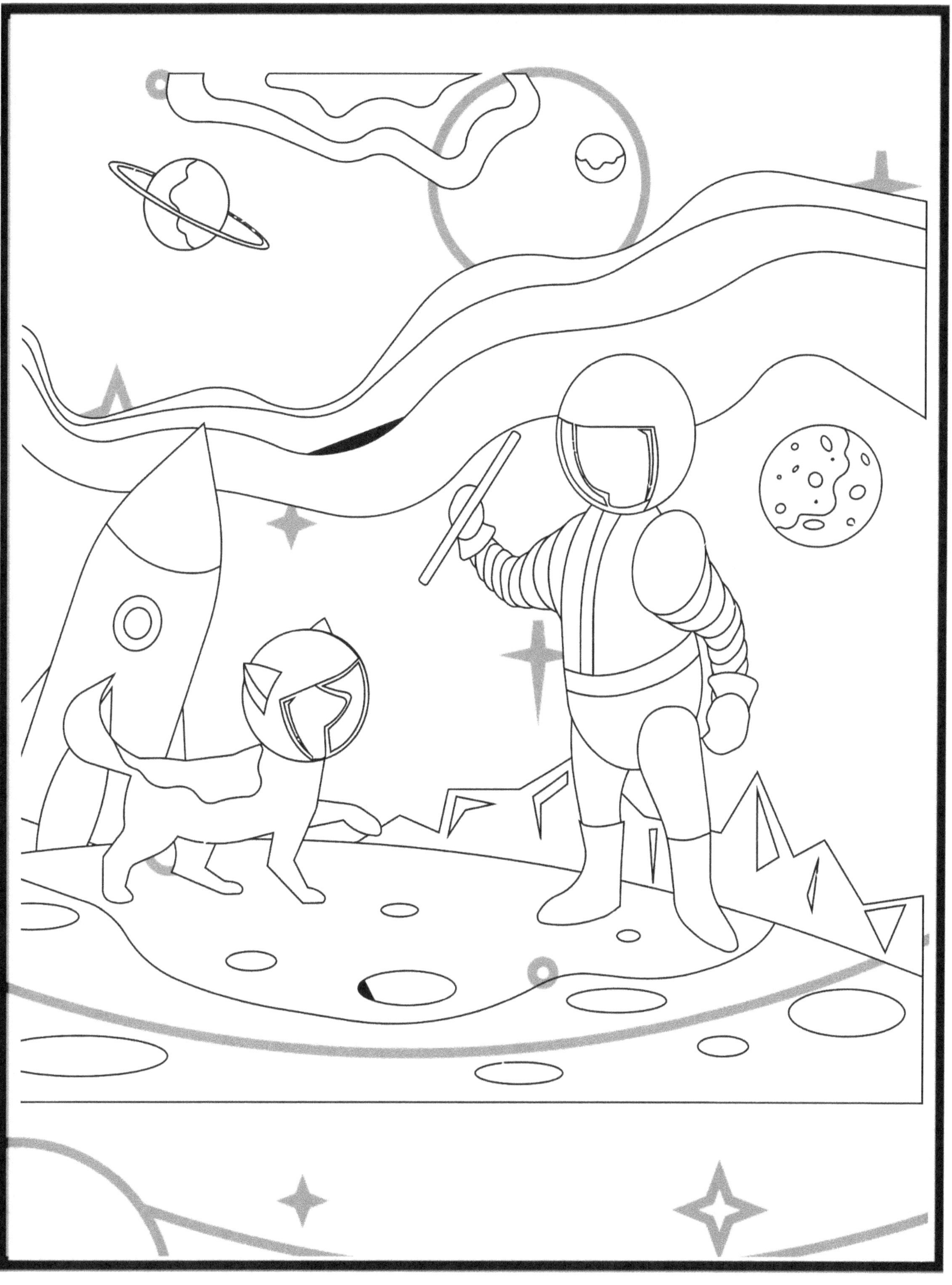

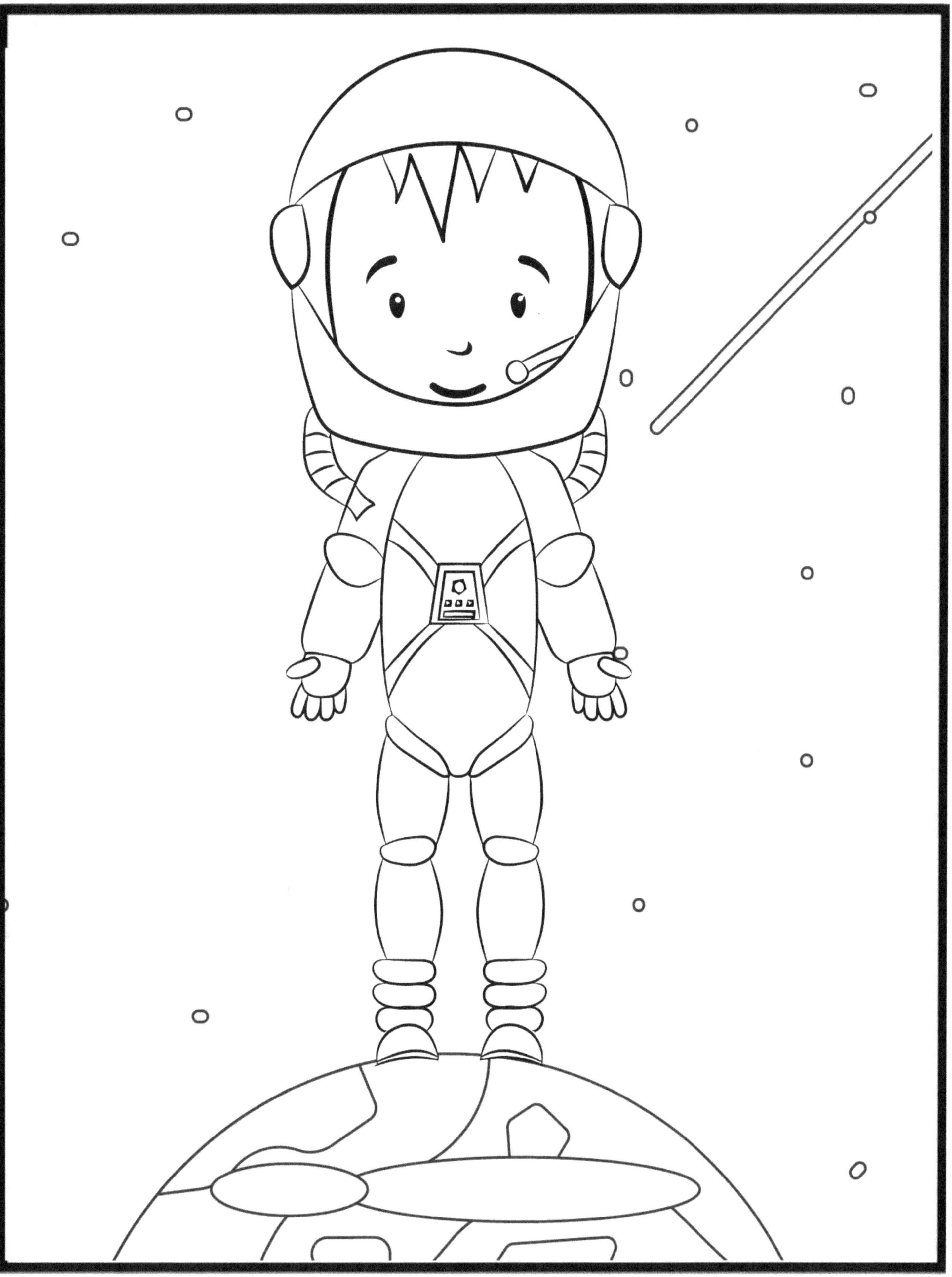

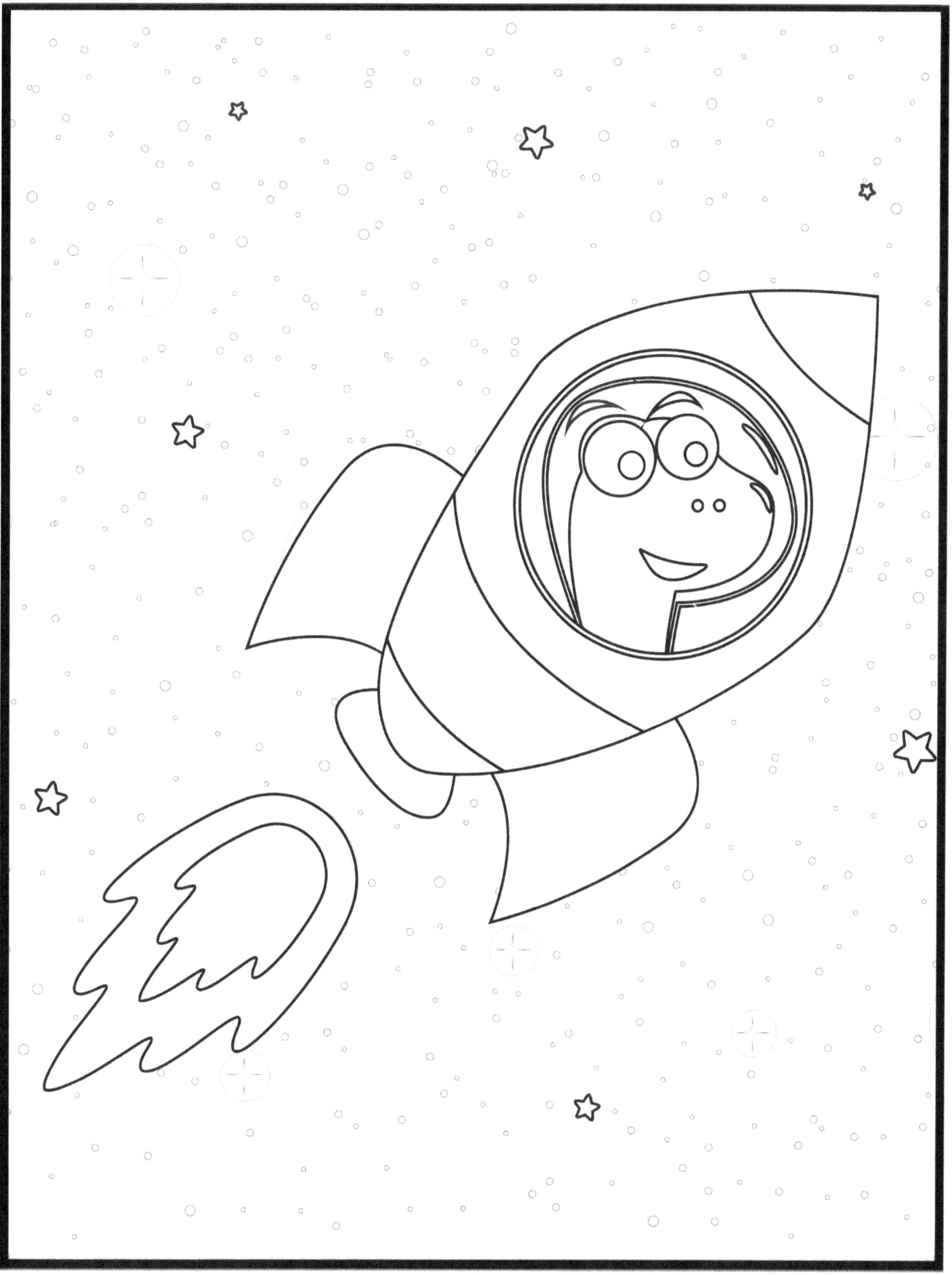

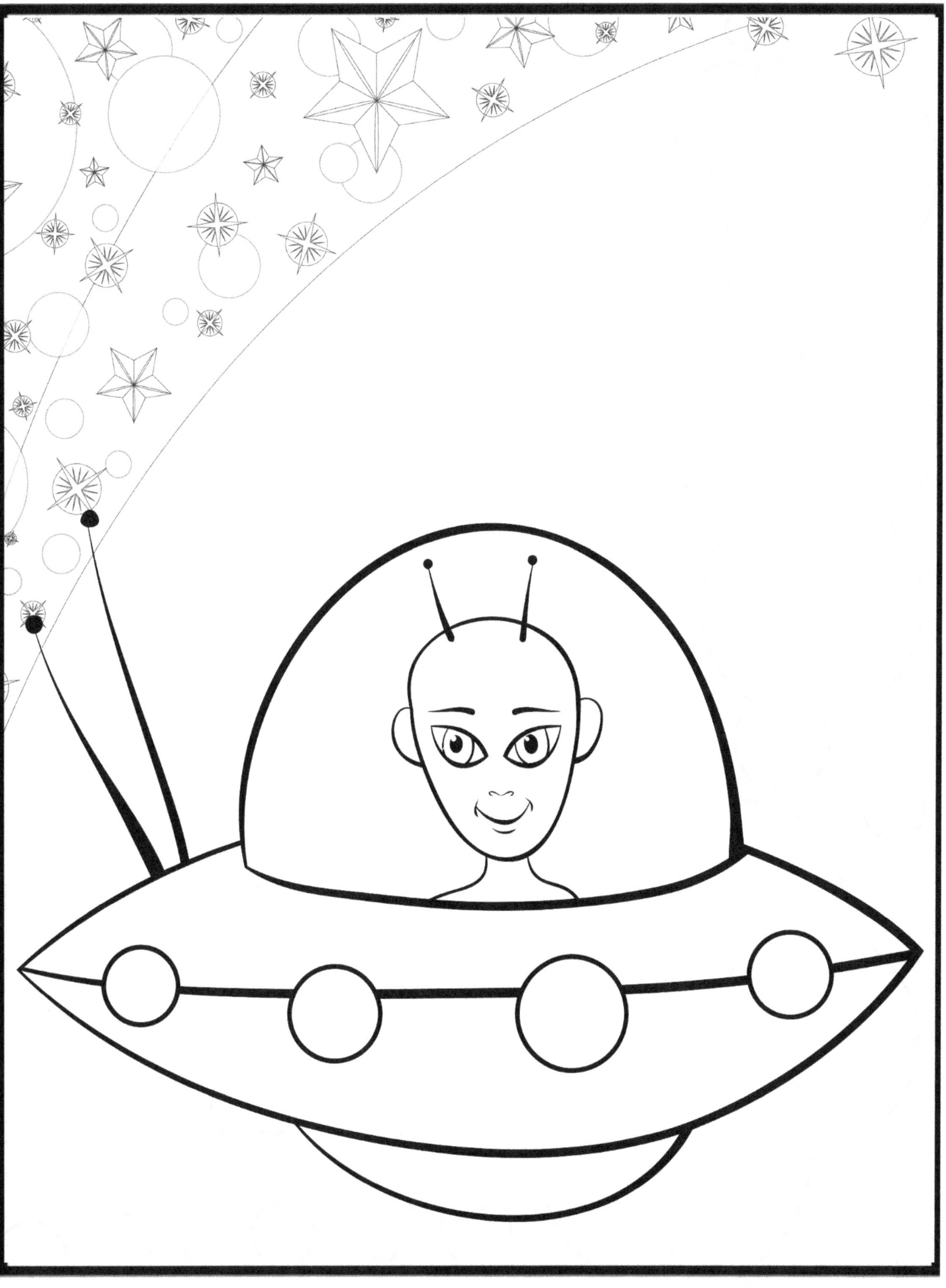

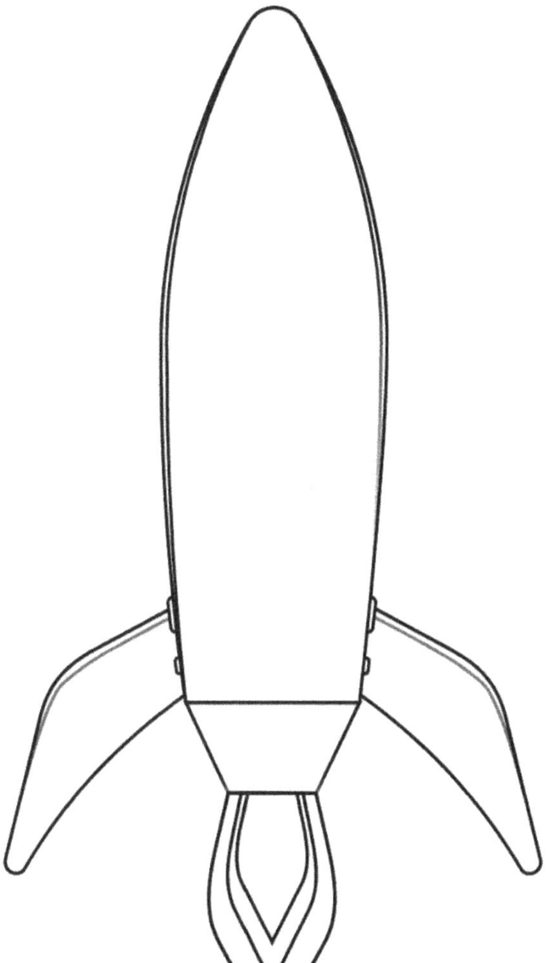
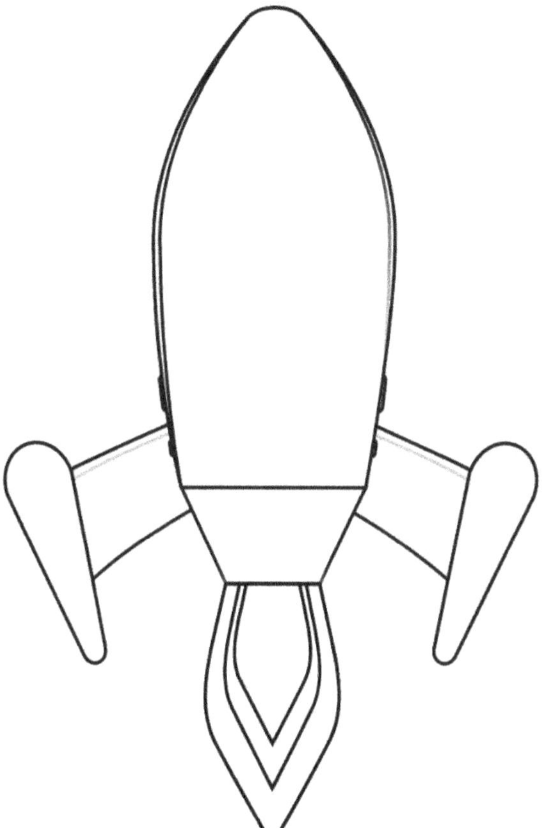

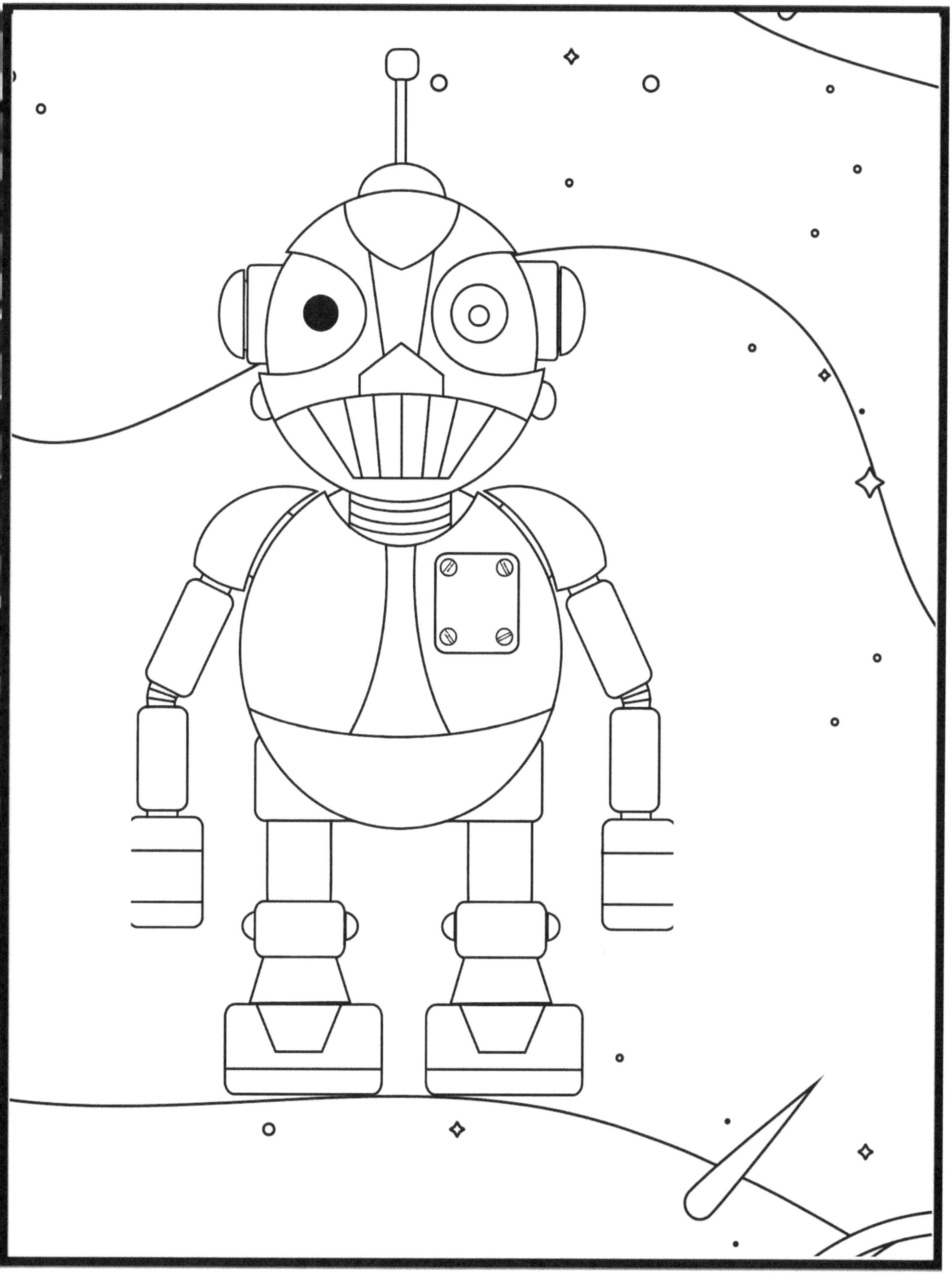

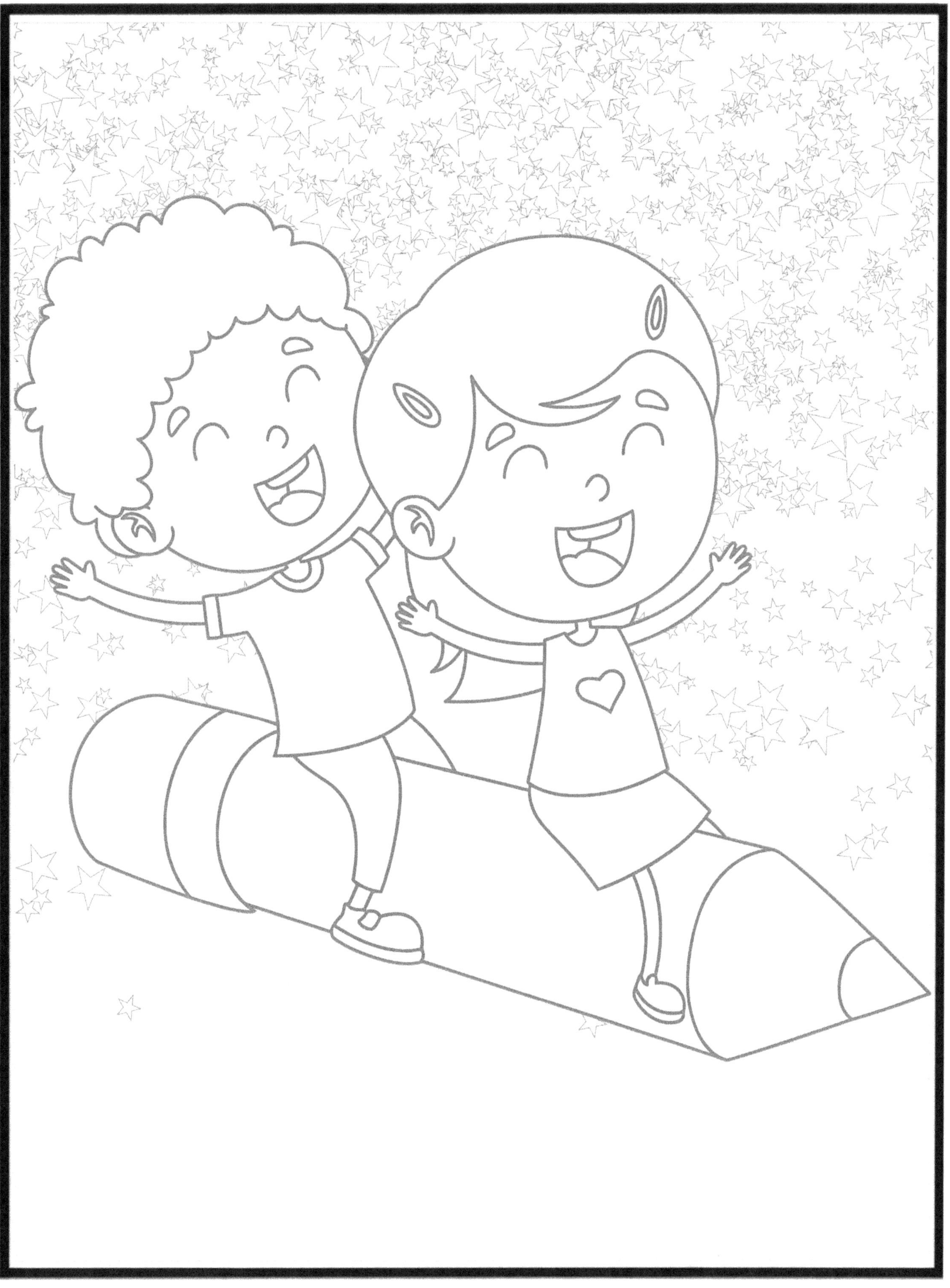

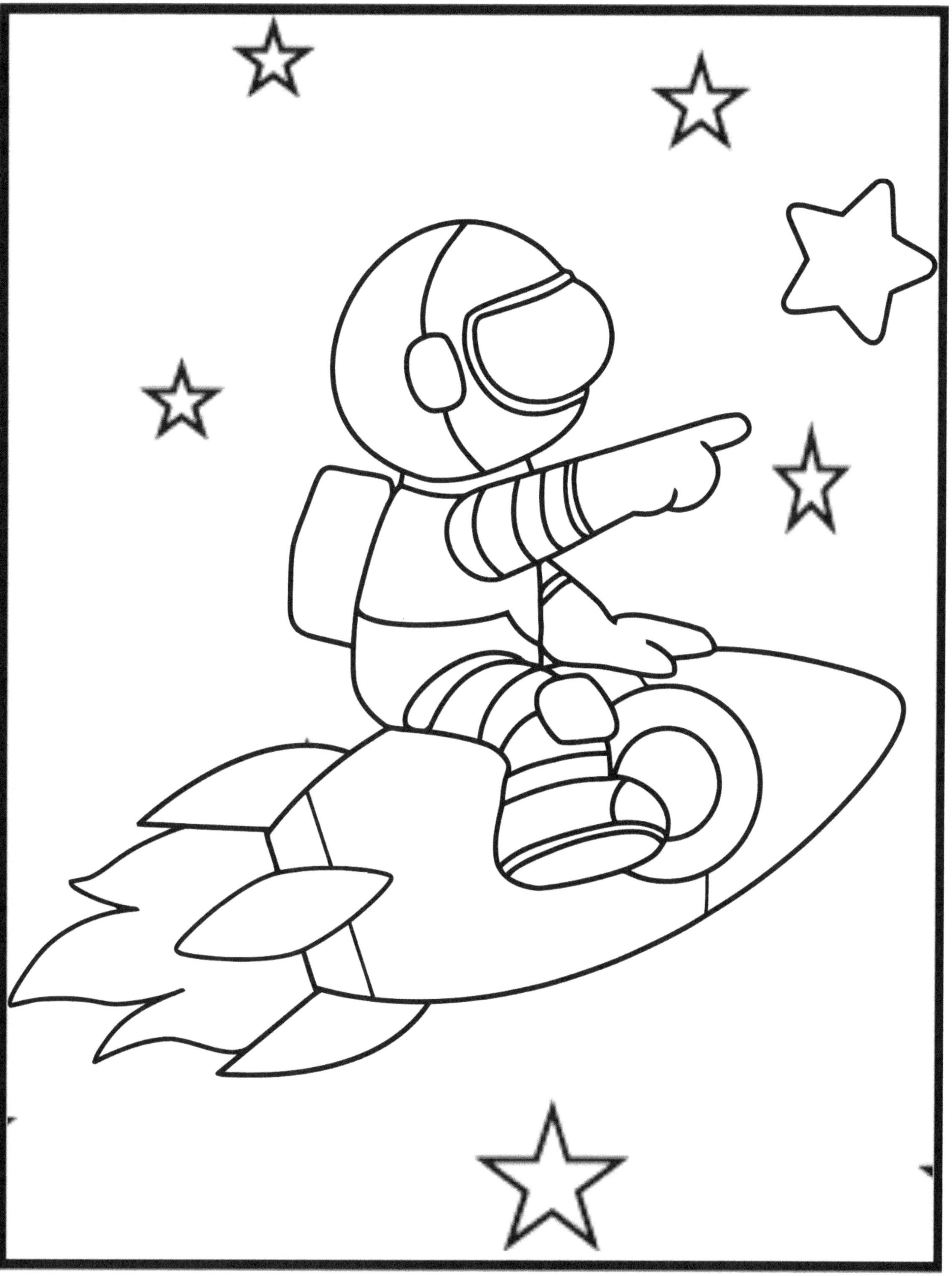

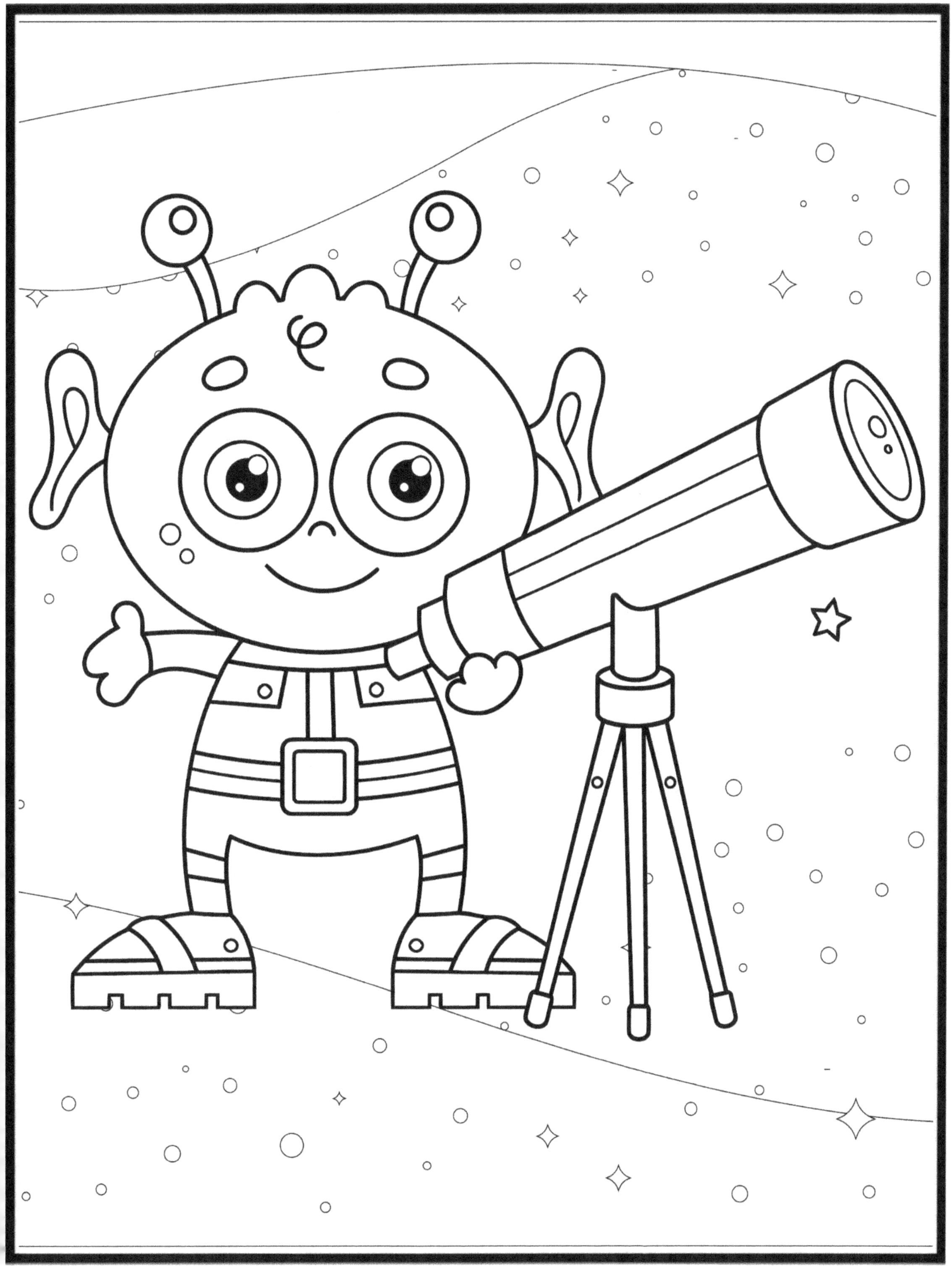

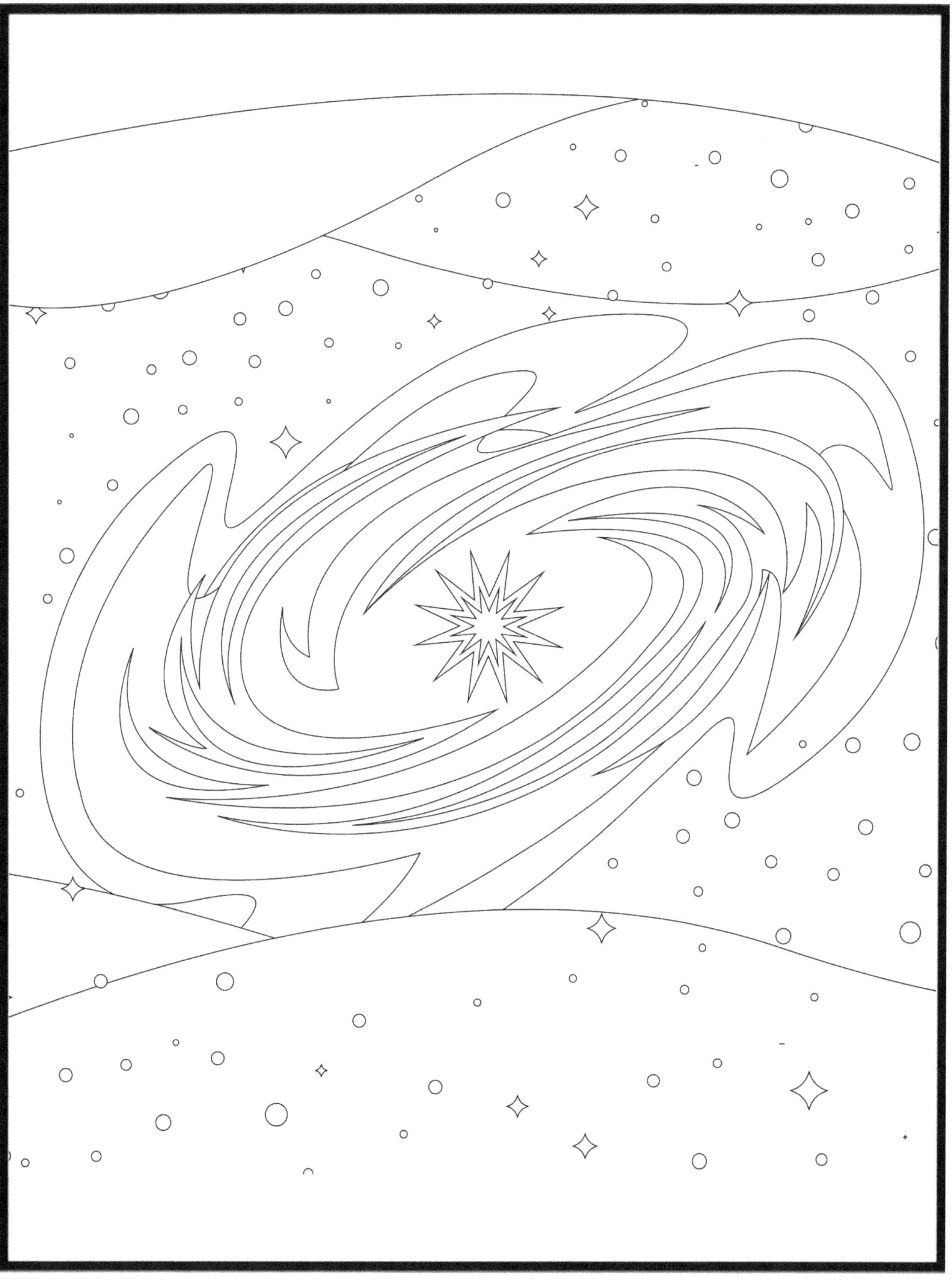

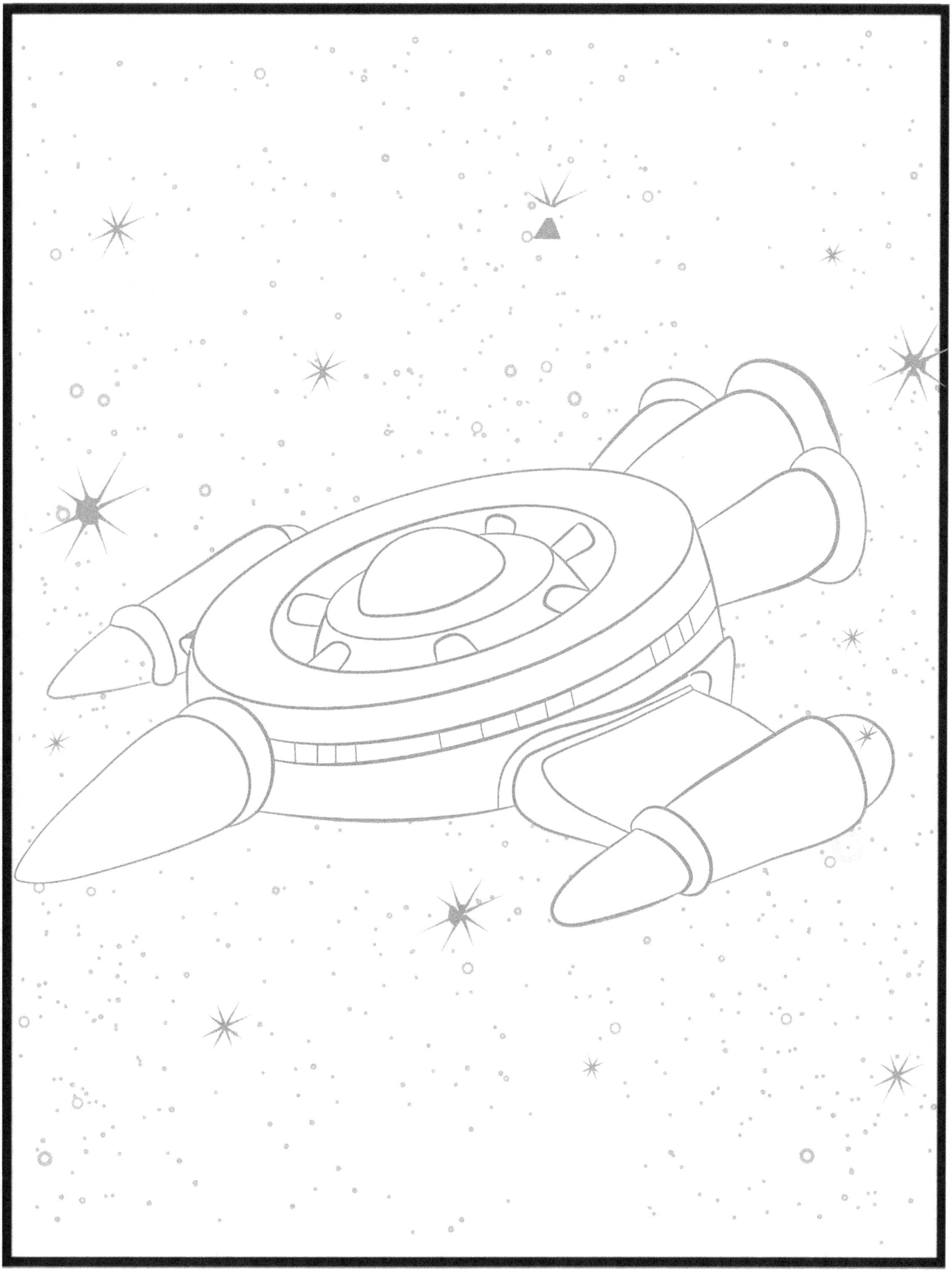

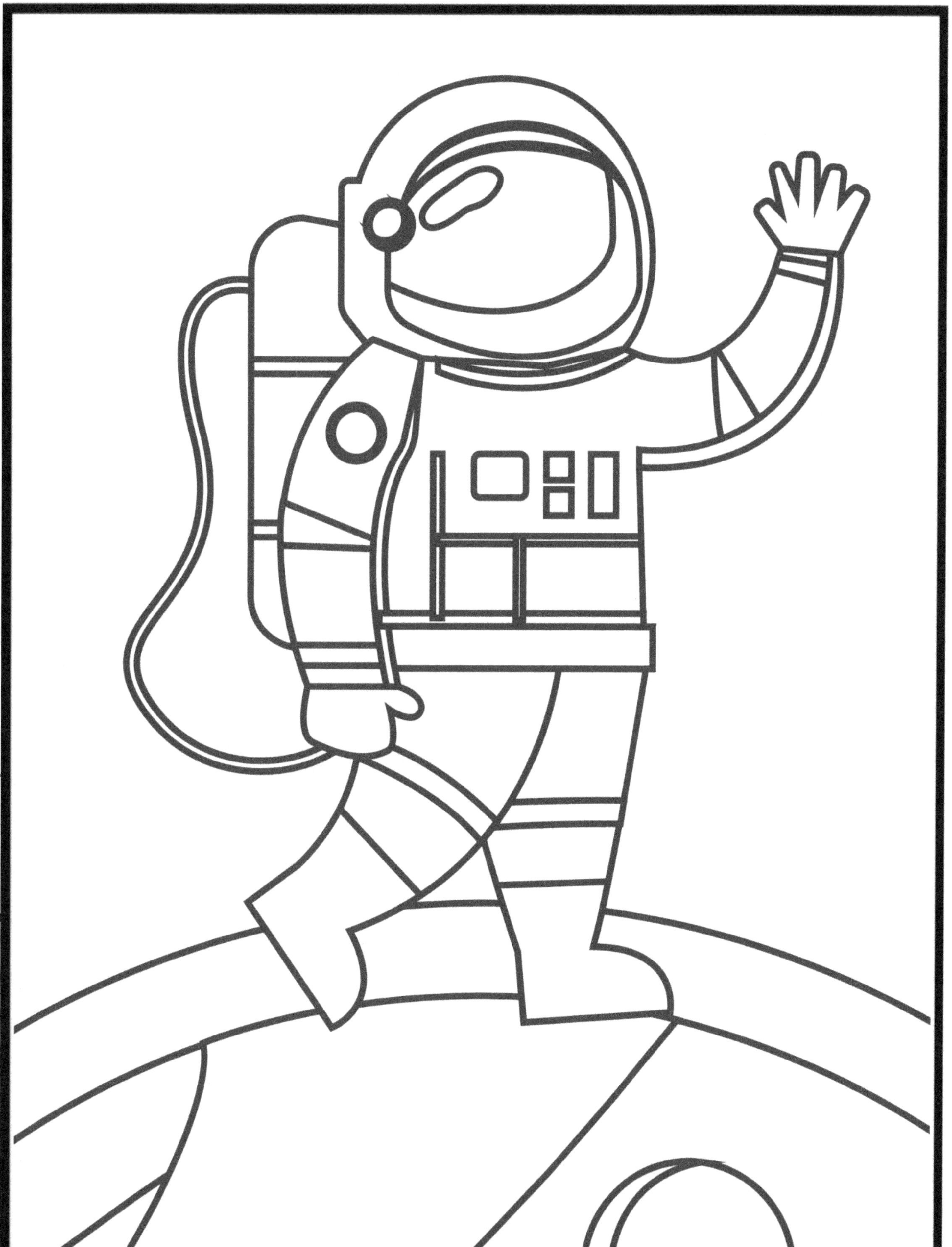

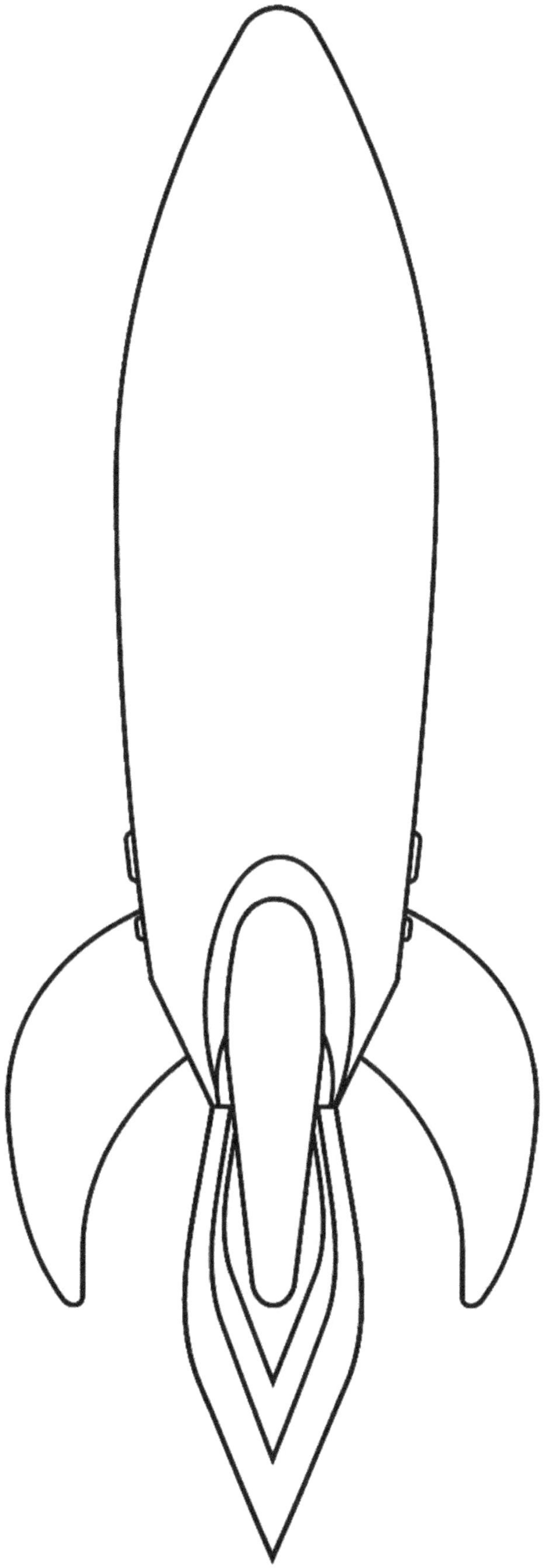

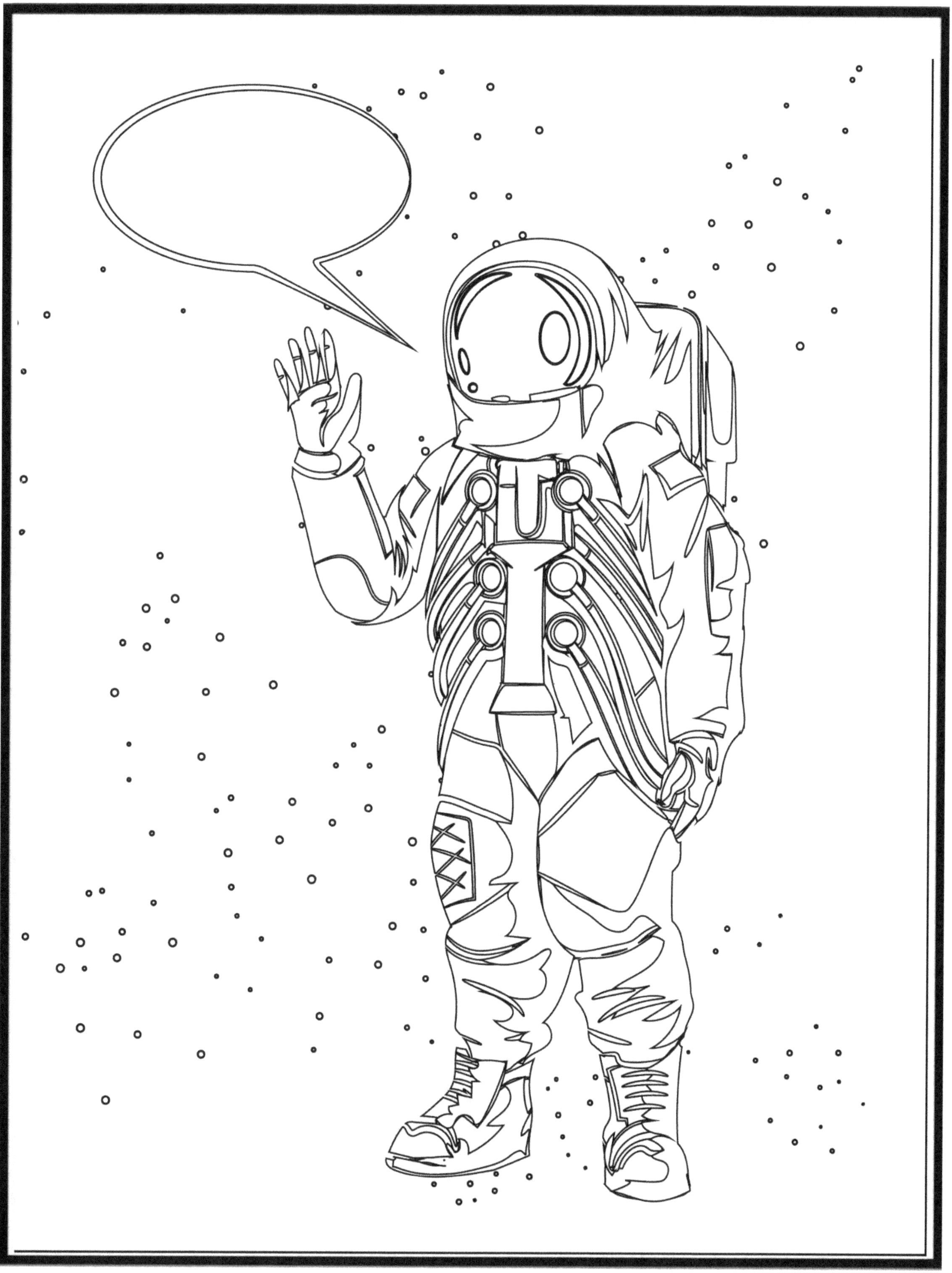

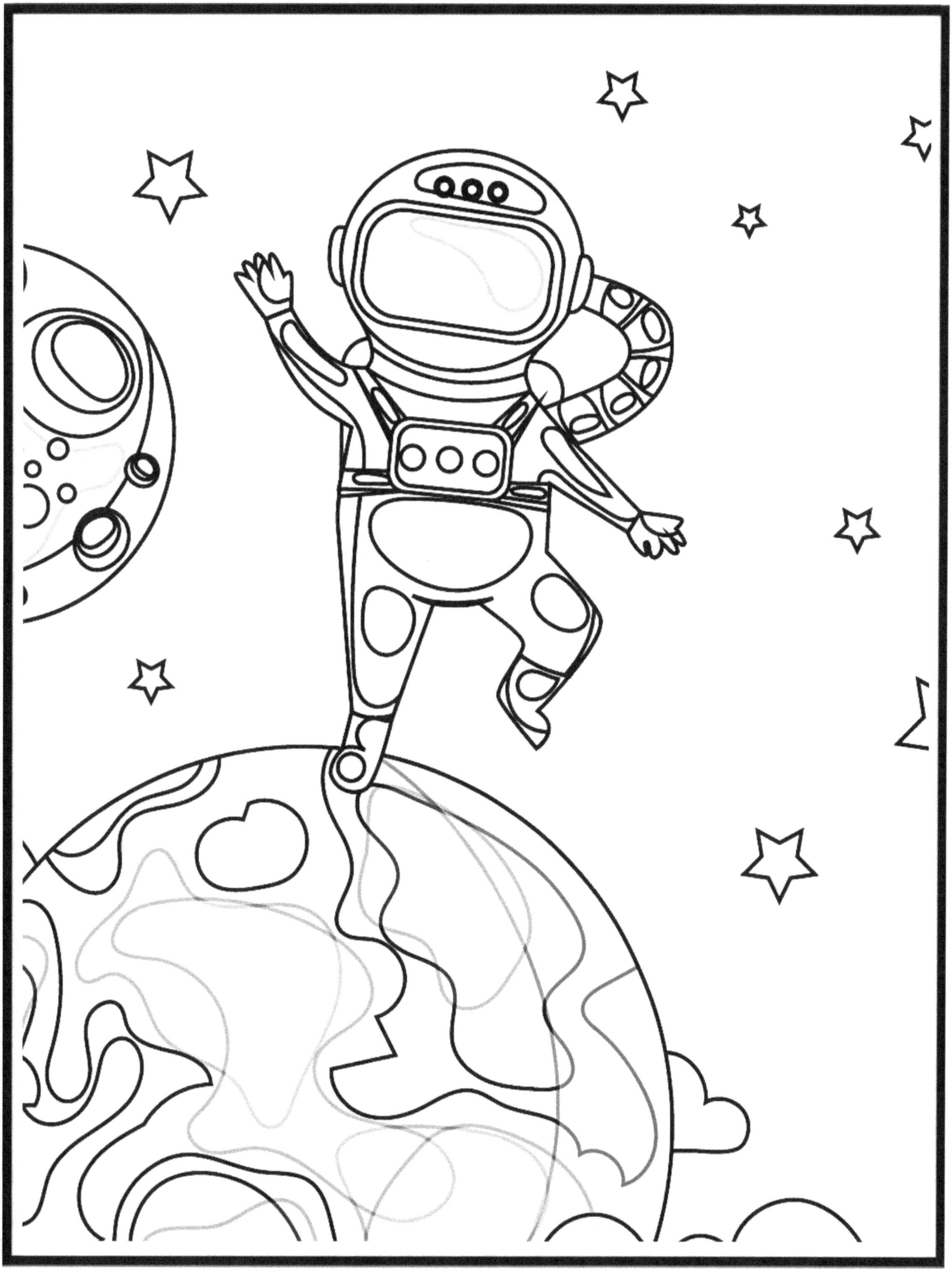

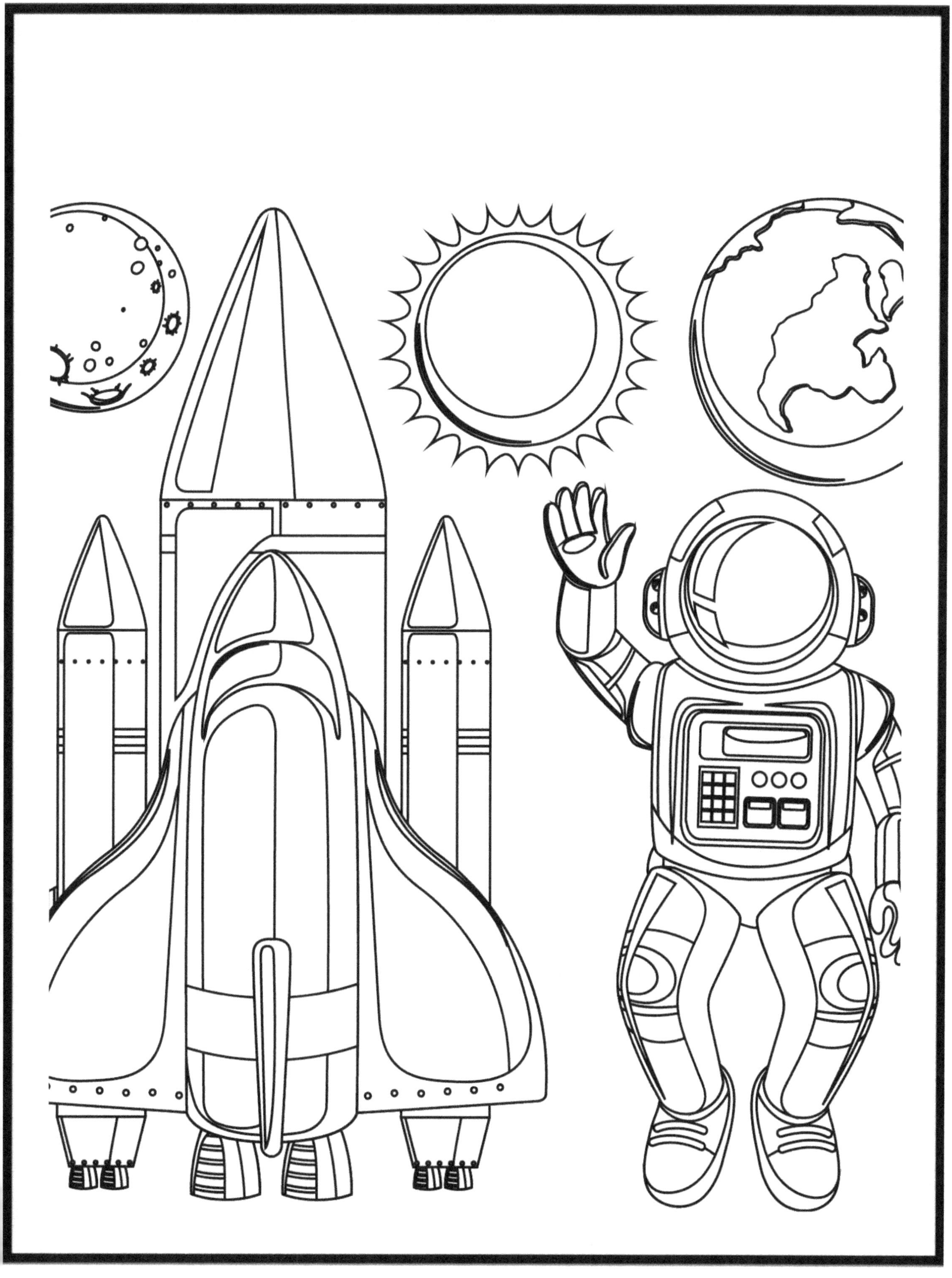

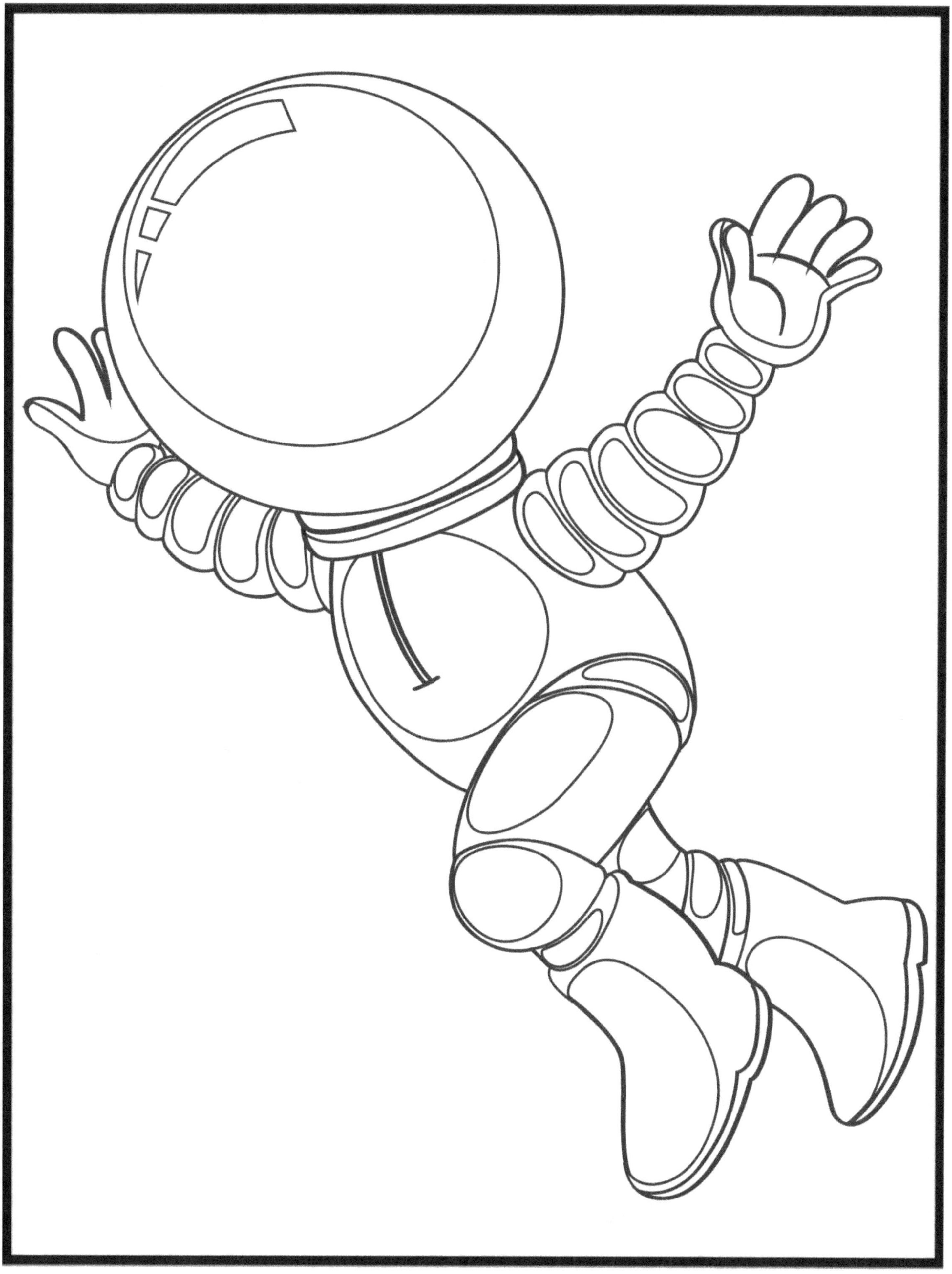